LIFE OF A HAUNTED HOUSE

The Barnstable House
of
Barnstable, Massachusetts

Poor Edmund Howes Lost all his money and this house

Genealogy of a
Real Haunted House

By Paul J. Bunnell, FACG, UE

HERITAGE BOOKS
2009

HERITAGE BOOKS
AN IMPRINT OF HERITAGE BOOKS, INC.

Books, CDs, and more—Worldwide

For our listing of thousands of titles see our website at
www.HeritageBooks.com

Published 2009 by
HERITAGE BOOKS, INC.
Publishing Division
100 Railroad Ave. #104
Westminster, Maryland 21157

Copyright © 2003 Paul J. Bunnell, FACG, UE

All rights reserved. No part of this book may be reproduced or transmitted in any form or by any means, electronic or mechanical, including photocopying, recording or by any information storage and retrieval system without written permission from the author, except for the inclusion of brief quotations in a review.

International Standard Book Numbers
Paperbound: 978-1-58549-859-8
Clothbound: 978-0-7884-8256-4

Special Remembrance

Corporal Benjamin Bonnell, U. E.

Without the spirit of Benjamin Bonnell, and the talents of Donna (Miller) Wyatt in 1985, this material would have never been written

Table of Contents

Preface		viii
Special Thanks Page		xi
Credits & Appreciation		xii
Introduction		xv
Chapter 1	1713	1
	1714	6
	Paines Buried in Barnstable	8
	Paine Family Genealogy	10
Chapter 2	The Little Girl, The Mother, And the Indian.	12
	1736	18
Chapter 3	Lemuel Shaw & Mr. Edmund Howes (c. 1776)	19
Chapter 4	Daniel A. Davis and Family	26
	Daniel Davis & Mehitable Lathrop Genealogy	32
Chapter 5	Doctor Samuel Savage	35
Chapter 6	Lemuel Shaw & Herman Melville	43

Chapter 7	The Many Faces & Names of The House	47
Chapter 8	First Hand Accounts (Encounters 1 through 10)	55
Chapter 9	Host for Eleven Ghost (Stories 1 through 9)	69
Chapter 10	1983 To 1985 (There's More) (Reports 1 through 4)	75
Chapter 11	Who Yah Gonna Call! 30 October 1985, 7:30 PM (The Day Before Halloween)	80
Chapter 12	Back Upstairs, For More Scares!	95
Chapter 13	A Bump In The Night	105
Chapter 14	Happy Halloween 1985	108
Chapter 15	Another Session At The House, December 1985	113

Chapter 16	Other Occurrences Before and After Halloween 1985 (File 1 through 5)	116
	The Legend Continues Today	122
	More Recordings	127
Chapter 17	Historical Facts About The Barnstable House (Owners & Renters Who Contributed To the Spirit of The House) (1 through 28)	130
Surname Index		137

Preface

This story would not have been investigated by this author without the influence of the 1985 discovery of some ghostly images on some photographs that were taken on top Devil's Back Mountain in Greenwich (Westfield), Kings County, New Brunswick, Canada during a genealogical research trip. A psychic (Donna Miller) read these photos at a psychic fair in Hyannis, Massachusetts. Shocking us over her findings that it was the spirit of my ancestor, Benjamin Bonnell, my interest went in that direction for a while. We later befriended Donna for several other research projects involving my first book, "Thunder Over New England, Benjamin Bonnell, The Loyalist."

Our relationship with Donna grew during the following months. Then, she invited us to attend a radio program at the Barnstable House one day before Halloween. We knew the house had a reputation of being haunted, but what we encountered that cold and windy night was so shocking and fascinating that this experience drove me to write this book.

Excited and overwhelmed by it all, my wife and I decided to devote time on researching the house based on our own past experience in genealogy. We dove into the history of the house, seeking newspaper articles, book reports, histories, genealogies, and interviews with eye witnesses. Placing all the material before me, I organized it in order by dates, births, deaths and events.

Suddenly, this very interesting story unfolded before me, and the only delay in the printing of this material was due to the many projects I had before it, which I apologize for.

Through the years I have become attracted to this old house. It's river of mystery running under it; the stories that surround it; and the history that lives in it. The house changed its name many times, but will always retain the name of "The Barnstable House" over all the others. In this book, I will use the name of "Barnstable House" to keep you focused on the story. From the first cutting of trees in Scituate, to the magnificent trip sailing on a wooden barge to Barnstable, and finally with its ghostly haunting. Are they real? I'm convinced

"If you find the sand dunes and salty air.
Quaint little villages here and there.
Your sure to fall in love with old Cape Cod."
Sung by Patti Page

Special Thanks

In Memory of Patricia D. (McCoy) White

Thomas R. Lynch, R. Ph.
Donna (Miller) Wyatt, Psychic
Matthew Paul Bunnell (Artist)

This Book is Dedicated To

Leslie Diane Bunnell
My wife

Who took part and supported this entire project

Credit & Appreciation

I would like to thank the many people and sources that helped supply the material to created this story.

Cape Cod Community College Library, Barnstable, Massachusetts.

The Sturgis Library, Barnstable, Massachusetts.

Donna (Miller) Wyatt, Psychic.

Cape Cod Times, Gwenn Friss, Hyannis, Massachusetts.

Barnstable, Three Centuries of A Cape Cod Town, by Donald G. Tryser, published by F.B. & F.P. Goss, Hyannis, Massachusetts.

Cape Cod Life Magazine, Resident Ghosts, The Haunting of Cape Cod, by Tim Wood (fall of 1984).

Yankee Homes, (October 1985 issue), Dublin, New Hampshire.

Guide to Old King's Highway Regional Historic District (bulletin) July 1983 (Extracted from a collection at the Sturgis Library, Barnstable, Massachusetts.

Credits Continue

Book Notes on Old House in Barnstable, by Francis William Sprague.

Barnstable County Court House (Deeds), Barnstable, Massachusetts.

The Barnstable Fire Department, 1975.

John G. Fitzgerald (once an owner), Sandwich, Massachusetts.

Cape Cod Times (front-page article), 1979.

Barnstable Patriot Newspaper, Hyannis, Massachusetts.

Craig Little (article written by him), 31 October 1982 (newspaper unknown), "More To Ghost Story Than Meets The Eye."

Journal of the History of Historic Mile, by Patricia Anderson, Marion Vuilleumier, Jack Frost, and Louis Vuilleumier, published by Tales of Cape Cod, Barnstable, Massachusetts.

Insight Newspaper, 19 December 1985, vol. 20, number 3, Barnstable High School, by Pamela Rymanowski and Michael Cox, Hyannis, Massachusetts.

Credits Continue

W.V.B.F., 105.7 Radio Station, The Lauren and Wallie Show, Boston, Massachusetts (A Halloween Special at the Barnstable House, 1985).

Chautaguan, The History of Barnstable County, Massachusetts, by Simeon L. Deyo, published by H.W. Blake and Company, New York, 1890.

The Dusty Rhodes Show, T.V. Channel 58, Hyannis, Massachusetts (27 October 1989 interview at the house with one of the firemen who witnessed a ghost).

Matthew P. Bunnell, who helped reconstruct the second visit to the Barnstable House in 1985.

Encouragement and support from Marion Vuilleumier, and the Professional Writer's of Cape Cod.

Robert Paine Carlson who has done much in preserving the gravestone inscriptions of Cape Cod on the Internet (http:www.capecodgravestones.com).

Introduction

The Life Of A Haunted House, The Barnstable House of Barnstable (Cape Cod), Massachusetts is a story of the entire life span of a haunted house. This story was also a very special and moving experience to this author and his family and friends. All the events that appear in this book are true and can be found in historical records, newspapers and libraries throughout the Cape Cod area. The first hand accounts of these sightings and happenings came from reliable citizens of the community including firemen. The Barnstable House is one of many famous haunted homes on Cape Cod. I dare you to read and believe this story!

Serving as a home, an Inn and a Hotel for almost three hundred years, this house has taken in much of the town of Barnstable's history including its people. Some for eternity! So, if you believe in ghosts, or not, the documentation and testimonies creating this story raise many questions to all of us regarding these spiritual entities. Do they really exist?

This story comes to life in 1713, and takes you right up to the present day. The birth of the house has been fictionalized, but based on true historical fact and records. Its occupants, living and dead drive this story through time. My desire is to record these accounts so the town of Barnstable has real facts on haunted history and genealogy of Cape Cod, keeping the exciting tradition of the Cape alive for all the Tourists seeking this kind of adventures, year after year. Let's not forget the year round residence that brings this story to life.

This town was founded in 1659 and many old homes were transported to the Cape in the same manner as this home was; by wooden barge.

The Barnstable House is now an office building with a few rental spaces available. The halls are more quiet, but for how long? Only time will tell if our ghostly friends from the past will soon appear again. They performed their finest feats when the peaceful life of the house returns to itself. This time is way overdue!

Chapter 1

1713

The village of Scituate located in the Commonwealth of the colony of Massachusetts was a very prosperous colonial town laying just a few miles south of Boston. A peaceful community in 1713 except for an occasional outbreak of Indian hostilities due to the white man who settled their lands. The Quaker's that lived there were a hard working lot, especially James Paine and his family. His ancestor, Thomas Paine helped build the town up by providing a few windmills around the Great Marsh at the mouth of the Marshfield River. The strong winds sweeping across the bay from the northeast turned the millstones and gave the villager's grains and flours, as well as tools to cut their wood so to make it easier to build their homes. These mills helped improved the quality of life for the entire area, giving them a trade, which was very important for their survival.

The Paines designed a fine house to be built in the coming year. They also planned 1to build a large barge to take it to "Shoal's Hope" which later became "Cape Cod." This stretch of land was around fifty miles to the south. James Paine had bought a few acres of land in a small, but prosperous village called Barnstable. Many of the early

Puritans were settling there. The shipping trade was becoming the main economic business and the family decided to get into that prestigious commerce.

The large trees in the Scituate forest would furnish the family the wood needed to build their new house, which would be later shipped down to Barnstable. In those days, the forest was thick and many Native Indian's still had control over them. It was their Garden of Eden as they played and hunted unlimited game there. They respected and loved nature, much more then the white man did. But, one day, the Paine's entered that forest causing two young Native's making love, to run for cover from the base of a large old tree. Several deer and rabbits also ran from the peaceful setting, all finally coming to stop at the edge of the forest.

Nothing would stop the white man as they kept conquering deeper into the forest. The natives and the animals from afar watched the several men approach the large tree. Glee suddenly glistened from their faces as three men encircled its trunk. They found it to be their choice for the Paine house. The two natives and the small animals watched as the day turned to disaster in the central forest.

Suddenly, a couple of careless colonists shot their guns in the direction of some birds that were fleeing the area too late. Several shots flew over head and both natives jumped to the ground shaking. Two birds lay dead not far from their feet. The two Indians leaped up and ran as fast as they could, stopping behind a large glacial rock. Both looked in the direction of the white men in the forest. A few other small animals followed them into the grasses for cover nearby. It didn't take long for the colonists to begin their noisy assault on the oldest tree there.

The white men slowly gathered around the tree. "Let us bring this one down," instructed Paine. As the large hatchets dug deep inter the trees flesh, only nature could hear the silent screams the enormous tree bellowed out. The rooted beast cried out to the sky knowing that its long existence was coming to an end. Of course no one listened, and soon loud cracks from the prehistoric monster were heard throughout the forest.

The crackling sound rang through the ears of the two Indian natives, and all the animals around took cover closer to the ground. Suddenly, the ground rumbled like an earthquake. Several deer could not stand by any longer and ran in fear. A flock of birds took flight into the sky. A terrible assault had befallen the forest. The mighty giant was down on the ground and the white men resurfaced from cover and checked out their prize.

They quickly went to work as several men started to carve up the carcass of the great one. Other men loaded the wagons or tied large ropes to horse teams to drag large pieces of the tree to the mill that lay along the river. History would soon show that the mighty tree would get its revenge!

The moment belonged to the Paine family. They carefully planned the construction of their future home. In a few months, the lumber began to pile up.

With a sawmill, the job was so much easier. Construction of the house began, but a very harsh winter slowed everything down, but soon a very mild spring arrived. The entire village came out to help complete the project of building the Paine house.

First, the frame was formed from the giant tree trunk. Several carpenter's began construction of a very large barge in the bay. The usual calm waters of Shoal's Bay would help it's building close to shore. Storms did develop quickly, but a keen eye would cry out any warnings during this project. The Paine's thought of everything. The only worry would be the trip on the barge to Barnstable. The weather had to be perfect.

The round logs traveled from the shoreline to the massive house that was now nearly completed. Many able bodied men showed up along with several strong horses to pull the structure along the logs to the barge waiting in the water. The entire town of Scituate came out to view the event. The mood was festive.

After a lot of hard labor, the launch went perfect. There were no injuries or mishaps. The house (and the tree) was now floating in the bay. The sails were let loose to the wind the house was soon on its way to a new home. The tree with its new form watched the shoreline of Scituate drift northward as the barge headed south to Barnstable. This was very unsettling to the tree. "Someone would surely pay for all this, it thought."

After a full days journey, the barge was sighted by some children playing in the Barnstable Harbor. Within minutes a large crowd gathered to greet and help the floating house ashore. The sight was a strange and eerie one as the sails of the barge surrounded the structure. The children found the event exciting. You don't see a house afloat in the bay everyday!

Scores of men waited with horses, wagon and logs. The wagons contained long thick cords that were made in Plymouth. They would soon be used to pull the house up the hill to the King's Highway in Barnstable Village.

The struggle of hauling the house off the barge was long and the uphill movement was much harder compared to the down hill direction at Scituate. Everyone pitched in and worked hard.

The house finally made it to the top onto the dirt highway. The movement became much easier, but still very dangerous and difficult. The Paine property was just down about a quarter mile. Their property was right on the King's Highway (Route 6A). The house foundation was already laid over an ancient spring. This practice was done to keep the Indian natives from poisoning the water supply of the White men during hostile attempts to drive the colonists off their lands.

The spring was rich in needed minerals that were necessary for life. The house already had different plans for this spring that would soon be under its foundation!

1714

The year was now 1714 as the Paines begin their new life in Barnstable. The walls of the house opened the first pages of its diary; an account that would affect the community for hundreds of years. The old tree felt strong again, but in a much different way. Its hold over the Paine home would soon take its place in history.

The following are true and real accounts of real people. Only the tree's point of view has been included. After all, he was the one cut down. Shouldn't he have the chance to tell his side of this haunting story? Come, and travel its hallways as history takes us through the inhabitants, their birth and deaths, their restless spirits as they lived and died in the **"Barnstable House!"**

Paines Buried in Barnstable

Many of the Paine family was buried at the Lothrop Cemetery which is located on Route 6A (The Old King's Highway) in Barnstable, Massachusetts. The front part of this cemetery has been destroyed from time and vandalism. This section was the oldest so many Paine's could be buried here. This author performed the research and publication of "Cemetery Inscriptions of the Town of Barnstable, Massachusetts and its Villages." This project has brought forth the following Paines buried here.

Bethiah Paine, daughter of the Honorable John Thatcher Esq., wife of James Paine, died 8 July 1734 at possibly the age of 63 or in her 63rd year. Her stone says: Here is buried Mrs. Bithiah Paine the virtuous wife and widow of Mr. James Paine dec'd daughter of the late Hon. John Thatcher Esq. She died July ye 8, 1715 Aetatis 63 (Marker has winged skull with narrow chin and a scroll border in the style of William Mumford or Nathaniel Emmes of Boston, stone cutters).

James Paine, located next to another James Paine (d. 1711)

James Paine, died 13 July 1711, age around 20 years. (I wonder what took his life so early an age?) He is next to the first James Paine.

James Paine, born 6 or 16 July 1665, died 12 Nov. 1728 or 18. Stone says: Here lies buried the body of Mr. James Paine born July 1665 and died Nov. 12, 1728. (The marker has a winged skull).

James Paine, died 1741
James Paine, died 1778(?)

Bethiah and the above James (b. 1665 d. 1728) were the builders of the Barnstable House. There is no documentation to date to prove that any Paine's exists in the spirit world in the house, but you can bet it took someone into its walls!

James Paine later became the grandfather of Robert Treat Paine, who was one of the signers of the Declaration of Independence, a proud legacy.

Courtesy of Robert Paine Carlson

Paine Genealogy

Thomas Paine
Married: Mary Snow

Children were: Lieut. Samuel Paine, b. c. 1652 Eastham, Ma.
Mary Paine, b. c. 1653 Eastham, Ma.
Capt. Thomas Paine, b. c. 1656 Eastham, Ma.
Eleazer Paine, b. 10 March 1658 Eastham, Ma.
Elisha Paine, b. c. 1658 Eastham, Ma.
Deacon John Paine, b. 14 March 1660/1 Eastham, Ma.
Child Paine (No dates)
Nicholas Paine, b. c. 1662/3 Eastham, Ma.

* James Paine, b. 16 July 1665 Eastham, Ma.
Joseph Paine, b. c. 1667 Eastham, Ma.
Dorcas Paine, b. c. 1669 Eastham, Ma.
* James Paine, b. 16 July 1665 Eastham, Ma. Died 17 Nov. 1718 age 53 at Barnstable, Ma. This family doesn't appear in Scituate, Massachusetts, but maybe they had business interests there? James moved to Barnstable around 1689. He was a school teacher, miller (Possibly this is where the lumber mill comes into play), cooper and a clerk. He was in Capt. John Gorham's company during the attack against Canada in 1691 as a clerk. For service, his heirs received a grant in 1736 of land in Maine. He was the first clerk of the East Precinct or Parish in Barnstable.
Married: Bethiah Thatcher, daughter of Col. John Thatcher (1639-) and Rebecca Winslow (b. 15 July 1643 -). Bethiah was born 10 July 1671 Yarmouth, Ma. And died 8 July 1734, age 62. Children were: James, Thomas, Bethiah, Bethiah (#2), Mary, Experience and Rebecca.[1]

---

[1] Though this family does not show up in Scituate, Mass., they are listed in the Sicuate Genealogy (http://babbage.clarku.edu/~djoyce/gen/scituate/rr02/rr02_213.html)

Chapter 2

The Little Girl, The Mother, And the Indian

Lucy was one of the first people to enter the house as a spirit. Stories, research and legends tell us that she was a lovely child between the age of eight and ten. She wasn't the first tragedy to strike the house or her family either. Sarah, her mother was a very private person and when she lost her husband to the "Davy Jones Locker", her life fell apart. Her little girl Lucy was the only sunshine in the house after that.

Sarah sat upstairs in her bedroom for hours each day, looking over the Barnstable Harbor which the house

---
which establishing them there around the time of the building of the
Barnstable House 1713. Children, Thomas and James are probably are builders.

commanded a fantastic view in those days. She stared out to hopefully see and prayed that she would spot the familiar sails surface over the horizon bringing her husband back to her and Lucy. She never believed the news that he was dead. Each day, her heart would sink deeper into death and her will to live was fading.

While feeling sorry for herself, Lucy was left alone to play and explore the depths of the house. No corner was untouched by her as she bounced her little blue ball everywhere. Each day when her mother disappeared upstairs Lucy's adventure began. The three stories of the house were indeed a large playground. The wicked eyes of the house watched her every move, waiting to take advantage of her coming fate.

Playful as always, Lucy carried her blue ball throughout the house, sometimes bouncing it real high. Other times just holding it to her side as she peeked around corners in her playful way. Rolling down the stairs was one of her favorite joys. The house was truly her playground.

"All but one area!" her mother instructed. Sarah forbid her to go down the narrow stairs to the earthen cellar where the underground spring surfaced. "Never go down into that cellar," Sarah demanded of her daughter. As most children, Lucy could explore only so far. The temptation of exploring the forbidden area was more exciting. Soon, the forbidden area became inviting and during one mid-day

Lucy knew her mother was upstairs sobbing over her daddy while looking for his sails to surface out over the bay.

This was her moment to travel down into the unknown. The dimly lit cellar! Because of all the taboo and rules to never go down there, the adventure was that much more. The thought was very thrilling and exciting to Lucy. Her approach to the cellar door was cautious. She noticed the narrow and dark the stairs. It was much different then her living quarters in the rest of the house. She could hear the basement breathing with excitement and anticipation. Finally, she descended the stairs with caution, but with a percentage of fear. Curiosity pulled her downward until her little bare feet touched the cold sand at the bottom. The earth was sandy and damp. Her candle flickered more from the drafts rushing about.

Soon, she heard it! The rushing of the underground spring. She walked over to its direction and found the water surfacing out of the ground at one end, and disappearing at another end of the cellar. The current was fast and swift. Lucy, still holding her candle in one hand and her blue ball in the other went to the spring's edge and sat down. She discovered her own playground and beach. "How could all of this be so bad, she thought."

Pushing the bottom of the candle into the sand freed one hand so she could play there. Tossing her ball up into the air gave her a big thrill. After a few moments of that she dug holes into the sand. "What a lovely place, she said to herself." She had plenty of time left on her candle, so she stayed down in the cellar for hours having the time of her life.

Upstairs, Sarah still sat in her lonely bedroom looking out the window for her lost, but dead husband never realizing where Lucy was playing. Lucy was having a great time in her new found world as she again, tossed her ball up higher and higher. Her next toss went even higher. So high that it went over her head. The ball tumbled down into the rushing water. There, it bounced about on the small waves as one end of spring shot it forward, while the other end tried to suck it into the earth. It kept bouncing back to the front of the stream.

Lucy tried to reach out for her blue ball, but couldn't find the inches to retrieve it. She knew one last stretch was needed to get her ball back. The house watched her every move, waiting for the moment to retrieve her soul. It did not take be too long before Lucy got to her feet and waited for the ball to bounce back to the out rushing water again.

She reached way out and suddenly lost her footing on the sandy shore. The earth gave way to the rushing water and Lucy fell into the cold rushing current. Crying out to her mother for help brought no response because of the distance between her and Sarah. It never allowed Sarah to hear her. The water was so cold that Lucy failed to hold onto the sandy edge. The icy conditions rendered her little body useless. Her screams for help sunk into the rushing currents below.

As the waters pulled her into the descending river and into the ground, her small lungs filled up with water. Her life was over, as we knew it. The body drifted through the spring tunnels taking her far away, but leaving her spirit behind, and in the house! The house had its first known victim as Lucy's blue ball suddenly splashed onto shore resting quietly for someone to find.

Soon after, Sarah came to her senses and noticed the vacant sounds of Lucy. She cried out her name and quickly started to explore the house for her. When entering the first floor from the stairs, she noticed the open cellar door across from her. Her face turned white and pale. She looked down to where the candle lit cellar below. She cried out Lucy's name. No reply, Sarah carefully went down the narrow steps to the tragedy below.

The neighbors, possibly the Davis and Sturgis families heard the loud screams coming from the Barnstable House. Sarah found her daughters blue ball and quickly went hysterical. It took all day to quiet Sarah down. The doctor gave her some herbs to help calm her nerves, but soon she was left alone in the big house. This time, to grieve over two. Soon after Lucy's memorial service, Sarah retreated back to the house; her eyes already darkened from the loss of her daughter. Draped in black, she ascended the stairs to her darkened bedroom where she immediately sat in her lonely chair for days. Soon after, she died there from starvation, loneliness and despair. The house took its second spirit.

The only record of a Lucy being possibly connected to the Barnstable House was a record of death of Mrs. Lucy Payne who was the consort of Mr. William Payne and daughter of Capt. William Taylor. She died 28 May 1776 in her 22nd. Year. Is it possible that they had a daughter named "Lucy?"
And the above named Sarah is really a Lucy? Only the house knows the truth![2]

---

[2] From Robert Paine Carlson collection.

1736

After 1736, the house took on another spirit. It is not known how or why. An Indian Native was reported to appear around the spring in the cellar. It was said that he was there to protect and guard the spring from any future tragedies. Was this brave also a victim of the spring? Or was he a victim of the white man before the house was built? Was he sent from above to stop any future deaths of children at the hands of the house? Today, these three spirits go about the house placing no harm upon anyone who they come across.

Chapter 3

Mr. Edmund Howes
(c. 1776)

Edmund Howes came from one of the oldest families who settled on Cape Cod (Shoal's Hope). Descending from Thomas Howes who came here in the sixteen hundreds and who was one of the first settlers of Barnstable, the family established a well-known reputation throughout the community. Edmund had inherited much from the family image and holdings. He was always fair and kind with his financial matters, but keeping a keen eye out for a good profit. Edmund wanted to climb higher up the ladder of success.

He soon got a chance to purchase the Barnstable House for a great price and possibly bringing him a large profit in the near future. This house would give him more prestige in the village. It is not known if Edmund ever heard any of the ghost stories of the house, let alone see any. The following events would soon thrust him into the spirit realm of this property and structure.

The British government was in need of more money and the heavy burden of taxation was already killing the financial pocketbooks of the colonies and Barnstable. People in the colonies were getting tired of financially supporting warfare throughout the world in the name of King George III. England was far away and the idea of separation became very popular. History soon had its way and the American Revolution was at hand. Barnstable became a beehive of activity as shipping became more important.

The opportunity for another investment came to Edmund and placing the Barnstable House up as security to invest heavily into this new business venture was needed. The investment was a sure thing and he planned to make a bundle on the deal. Now, only thirty-seven years old, he waited for the biggest transaction in his life to go through. It was 1777, the second year of the Revolutionary War; Edmund put up the Barnstable House, as security. He changed it all into cash and waited for the big day to arrive.

When it came, Edmund gathered up his life long savings and went down to the docks to enter into the venture. He quickly found his partner, the one who promised to double his fortune. He placed his name on the contract to seal the agreement. He also cashed in all his other holdings leaving him very vulnerable. This was a very risky step.

Edmund, smiling, placed all his Continental money into his partners
hands, eager to get his cash holdings into work. He looked up at his partner's face and waited for his excited reply. The partner looked down at all the bills and slowly raised his head and gazed into Edmund's bright eyes.

"My God man! I cannot accept this money! Haven't you heard? These bills are worthless! Continental bills are no good anymore! Is this all you have?"

Shocked over what the man said, Edmund looked cautiously down at his entire fortune. They were in deed Continental bills. His blood ran cold from his face. He never said a word to his partner. He slowly placed the worthless money back into his bag and slowly disappeared up the hill to the King's Highway. He was in shock beyond belief. He walked back to the Barnstable House that was now owned by someone else. An old gentleman saw Edmund from across the street and yelled out; "Are you alright?"

Edmund did not answer the old man. He kept walking a death march towards the house. He thought how fast his money went bad and how he lost everything. The war had destroyed his entire life as he saw it. In a daze, he reached the house, opened the door and entered as if it was still owned by him. The house watched his every move. Edmund found a chair and sat there for hours still gripping his life savings in his hands.

Finally, he slowly got up and went to the back of the house that faced the bay. He reached for a long rope hanging by the back door. Walked to the back yard where he found an old tall oak tree. The house continued its watch in glee as it waited for Edmund's final move.

The poor distraught man threw the rope over the strongest limb and climbed up onto another. He looked at the rope as it swung around for a few seconds, fixing his eyes at the center of the noose he had just made. Finally, getting enough nerve, he reached out and grabbed the rope and placed it over his head. In one last desperate protest, he cried out to the heavens, and then he jumped to his death.

The fall was quick, breaking his neck instantly be snapping it just under his right ear. His body jumped about for a few seconds as every nerve sent out the last remaining messages of despair. Now hanging there quietly, the cool sea breeze blew his hair around his head, and the worthless money laid below him starting to blow into the wind.

The neighbors soon found his body and placed it into a wagon, taking him to the undertaker. Another death had befallen the Barnstable House and another spirit now walks the hallways with the others. The belly of the house was getting full, but the pains of the past still cried out for more victims.

The only pre-Revolutionary Howes found in the town cemetery records were:

Desire Howes, died 11 Jan. 1822 in her 75th. year which would have placed her birth around 1767. She was the widow of Peter Howes. She is buried at the Sandy Street Cemetery located on Route 6A in Barnstable

Peter Howes, died 27 Nov. 1800, age 58, which would have placed his birth around 1742. He to is buried at the Sandy Street Cemetery on Route 6A in Barnstable.

There was an Edmund Howes in 1679 who served on the Select Court in Yarmouth. Could he be an ancestor to Edmund? An Edmund Howes who also served as a representative in 1780 is listed. There was also an Edmund Howes who served as a Chatham Selectman for 4 years starting in 1707. All the above towns are just a few miles apart.

There is a notation found in the History of Barnstable County of some Howes who owned a tavern; "The present county road forms the principal street of the village, and along it the early ordinaries were found. Where Mrs. Moses Howes now lives (1890) was an old fashion two-story tavern, kept by Joseph Hall before 1784. About the same time there was a tavern kept by Obed Howes, where Harvey Howes now lives (1890). Obed Howes father, called "Great Sam," had kept it prior to Obed. Henry Hall's tavern with its sign of a black horse, was opened just prior to 1800, and stood where Howes Chapman now lives (1890).

All the above listed Howes descend from Thomas Howes.

There is an Edmund Howes listed in the World Family Tree CD collection, volume 3, Pre 1600 to Present Day records who was born 10 April 1742, married 11 Feb. 1773 to Abigail Crosby, born between 1734-1756 and died between 1778-1845. This Edmund died between 1788-1833, which places him into the window of time mentioned in the above account. He was also the son of Thomas Howes, born 1673, son of Ebenezer, born 20 June 1699 and his mother was Deborah Sears, born between 1688- 1794 and died between 1837-1889. She was the daughter of Paul Sears, born 1647-1765 and Mercy Freeman. Records from the UA Hintze, Automated Family Pedigrees #1 CD 100 collection listed the marriage in 1764 in Yarmouth, Massachusetts between Edmund and Abigail. There are no children listed. There are discrepancies in some of the above records.

Another record[3] of Thomas A. Howes says birth 22 Jan. 1700, Yarmouth, Barnstable County, Massachusetts; death 12 Nov. 1764, Dennis, Barnstable County, Mass; buried at Old Burying Ground, Dennis, Mass. He shows as being the son of Ebenezer Howes and Sarah Gorham. Thomas wife is listed as Deborah Sears

---

[3] http//www3.simpatico.ca/daconway/d0001/g0000018.htm

This possibly the same Edmund Howes is listed as birth 10 Aug. 1743 and death 10 Sept. 1828 at Hawley, Franklin, Massachusetts at age 85. His parents are different from above. They were Amos Howes, born 1706 and Rebecca Matthews, born 1714. He is shown as being married to Abigail Crosby, born c. 1741. They had a child named Molly Howes. If this record is correct then this Edmund is not our unfortunate subject listed above.[4]

---

[4] From htt://history.vineyard.net dated 2002.

Chapter 4

Daniel A. Davis and Family

Shortly after Edmund Howes death, the Davis family moved into the house giving it its first officially known name; "The Davis House." They quickly remodeled and cleaned up the place along with expanding it. At this time, their neighbors were Captain E. Crocker, Mrs. L. Smith, J. T. Hall, R. W. Waitt, E. Smith, Captain J. T. Holt and H. C. Everett Farnes.

Daniel A. Davis owned the house from 1777 to the mid-1790. It could be possible that Davis acquired the house through Edmund Howes misfortune. Any real stability came after this family moved it. His son was born on 7 October 1745 and was a doctor living first in Eastham, now Orleans. He became very successful, and was the Judge of the Probate Court in 1800 after moving back to Barnstable. He died on 27 May 1825 at the age of 80. Research has not established him as any spirit who lives in the house.

The owner, Daniel Davis served as a Barnstable Selectman in 1756 and on 16 Nov. 1774, he was appointed to a committee to communicate with other counties along with Colonel Nathaniel Freeman, Joseph Otis, Thomas

Paine and Job Crocker. This appointment was by the County Congress, which was held at Barnstable and headed by the Honorable James Otis who was also the moderator.

On 11 October 1775, Daniel was appointed Judge of Barnstable by the governor, and the people of Massachusetts, and was made an incumbent Judge on 27 March 1781. He was very active during the revolutionary war. The above mentioned committee under James Otis housed its headquarters at the Sturgis House, just a few doors down from the Barnstable House. The group who were most ardent men in the cause of freedom and Daniel filed charges against the Loyalists with Joseph Otis and fourteen others on 26 June 1776. Also listed on this committee were; Thomas Paine, Captain Joseph Doane and Captain Jonathan Howes, surnames well acquainted with the Barnstable House. Their patriotic duties and values ran extremely high in caliber.

After 1777, the family did sight a few ghosts in the house. Fearing them dearly, they sought refuge with their pastor who headed the Congregational Church in West Barnstable. The family fled there for a while. No prescription was given, but the family knew that the subject of ghost should not be brought up again. They went back to the house and quickly faced the facts that they all had to live together with the harmless spirits floating about. They made it a point to stay clear of them.

Daniel Davis soon purchased a small parcel of land across the King's Highway (Route 6A) across from the Barnstable House. He too invested heavily into the community and watched for every opportunity to come along. Having high standards, his family elevated to great recognition in the village and Cape Cod.

There was one occasion that he found quite amusing and told his family about it. It involved himself during the American Revolution, and George Thacher of Yarmouth who were both fifes during this time. They were both stationed at Lexington when they got orders to return home. On their way, they stopped off at Marshfield, Massachusetts to rest. The trip was long and their feet were killing them both.

Being so disgruntled, they broke into a Farm, opened the barn door, and spotted a horse. They quickly saddled him up and rode off into the night, stealing the farmer's animal, which was a very high crime back in those days. The farther they rode, the more sore and weary they got. They committed a crime and it was too late to do anything about it. Their desires for an easy ride home placed them in grave danger. Stealing a horse was a major offense, even death.

Years later, when both men were much older and George Thacher was a Judge of the Justice of Supreme Court, he was presiding at a session in the county of Kennebec, (Maine), then part of Massachusetts, a horse thief was on trial and the Commonwealth's solicitor general was Daniel Davis Jr. himself; his old horse thief buddy of long ago. He was prosecuting the poor chap in this case and during a lull in the proceedings, the Judge leaned over the bench and whispered to Daniel, the prosecutor;

"Davy, this reminds me of the time you and I stole that horse and rode to the Cape with."

Daniel Davis, first elected in 1752, was a selectman of Barnstable for twenty-three years. The above is his account, approved by town meeting, for attending congress at Salem, Cambridge, Concord and Watertown during the Revolutionary period.

Copy of original war accounting documents for payments to Davis.

    The Davises were a colorful family and their duty to their country and community was very strong. The ghosts continued to appear to them, but they refused to accept them or report them fearing that their reputation would be tarnished. The Honorable Daniel Davis Esquire died 22 April 1799 in his 86th year.

Top half of Daniel Davis gravestone at Cobbs Hill Cemetery

Daniel Davis & Mehitable Lathrop Genealogy

Robert Davis Born c. 1628   Died 1693
Married: Anna Born c. 1630   Died 1701

Son: Joseph Davis   Born 1662
Married: Hannah Cobb Born 28 March 1671
            Died 3 May 1739
     Daughter of James Cobb Born 14 Jan. 1634
              Sarah Lewis Born 2 Feb. 1643
                   Died 11 Feb. 1735
Children: Robert Davis   Hannah Davis
      Joseph Davis   Mary Davis
      Gersham Davis   Lydia Davis

Son: Daniel Davis Born 28 Sept. 1713,
    Barnstable, Massachusetts
    Died 22 April 1799, Barnstable,
    Massachusetts
    He is buried at Cobb's Hill Cemetery in
    Barnstable.
    His stone reads:
    "Reader, be encouraged by his example to
    the practice
    Of industry, temperance, piety and
    patriotism and
    Your reward like his shall be long life, the
    esteem of
    The wise and good in this world and joyful
    hope
    Of a happy immortality beyond the grave."

Married: Mehitable Lathrop   Died Nov. 1764,
    Barnstable, Massachusetts
    Daughter of Thomas Lathrop
    Born 6 Jan. 1673 Died 3 July 1757
    And Experience Gorham Born 24 July 1678
    Died 23 Dec. 1733

Children: Mary Davis
Daniel Davis
Robert Davis
John Davis
Deborah Davis
Thomas Davis
Experience Davis
Mehitable Davis
Lathrop Davis
Daniel Davis
Desire Davis
Ansel Davis[5]

---

[5] Listed genealogy from Daniel Davis and Mehitable Lathrop genealogy http://www.cybertrails.com dated 2002.

Chapter 5

Doctor Samuel Savage

Probably, the strangest person to ever live in the Barnstable House was Doctor Samuel Savage. A very peculiar man, he lived there for a short time entertaining many people with his very different personality. Some say it was because he had extremely high intelligence. By 1799, Dr. Samuel Savage owned the Barnstable House according to one source. Another source said he was renting from another family member. He did earn the title of "Medical Patriarch of Cape Cod."

Born 11 August 1748 to Samuel Phillips Savage and Sarah Tyler in Boston, they quickly discovered that their child was very bright. Without giving the young Samuel a choice, they started to plan his life out. Baptized at the Brattle Square Congregational Church, they confronted an official there and discussed their child's future plans. When he became of school age, he was enrolled at the Boston Latin School, later he graduated with an A.B. degree from Harvard College in 1766, and taught at the Lincoln and Weston Town schools for several years. He went back to Harvard and conferred his A.M. degree in 1777. He received his medical training by preceptorship from Doctor Benjamin at the Church of Boston and soon became the Surgeon General of the American Army.

He settled on Cape Cod in 1772 and in January of 1775, the East Parish of Barnstable delegated him to deliver ten shillings as a donation to the besieged Boston. On 6 Sept. 1778, he signed up to serve four days of military duty because of a British attack on Bedford, Dartmouth and Falmouth, Massachusetts, serving in the Massachusetts Militia headed by Captain George Lewis in Col. Nathaniel Freeman's Regiment.

Samuel was elected as Fellow of the Massachusetts Medical Society in 1786, and retired from that position after thirty-four years. He was listed in the Journal of the History of Medicine and Allied Sciences, Inc., by Fred B. Rogers[6]. Is listed as a long time medical practitioner on Cape Cod and remembered for his wit and character. A Yankee individualist who lived in a stern era

He married Hope Doane who was the daughter of Col. Elisha Doane and Hope Rich of Welfleet, Massachusetts on 18 February 1777. She was born in 1756, and died in 1830. Their life was very successful, but not a happy one. Tragedy followed them everywhere. This could be another reason why Samuel was so bazaar.

---

[6] Found at the Sturgis Library Ref. 929.2 Sav Rog Lothrop Rm.

They had three sons; William, Joseph and Tyler. All three died in their infancy. They had three more sons who died in their early manhood. John, a law student who graduated from Harvard in 1810 died at the age of twenty-two. The following year, his brothers, Elisha and Samuel died at Kingston, Jamaica where they were living, trying to improve their fragile health condition. A seventh son, Charles became a United States Council to the Republic of Central America, stationed in Guatemala City from 1825 to 1838. He married Susan Wood who was the daughter of General Abraham Wood of Wiscasset, Maine. She was born in 1790, and died in 1825, not living a long life.

Samuel's only daughter was Hope Savage who was the second wife to the Chief Justice, Honorable Lemuel Shaw who was born in 1781 in Barnstable, and died in 1861. He was the Chief Justice of the Massachusetts Supreme Court from 1830 to 1860. Hope had two sons, Lemuel and Samuel. She died in 1879. Through her stepdaughter, Elizabeth Shaw, she was the mother-in-law of the novelist, Herman Melville.

Samuel Savage became the Clerk of Common Pleas for Barnstable in 1782, and eight years later became the Justice of the Peace. In 1815, he was also appointed to the Quorum. He died on 28 June 1831 at the age of eighty-three.

When he lived in the Barnstable House, he walked about town attracting much attention, giving every neighbor such a show. He had a striking appearance that made everybody turn his or her heads to notice him. If that didn't work, his loud shouts would surely do the trick. Often, he talked to himself as he wondered around. Maybe he was an excellent candidate for conversing with the spirits of the house?

A John Thacher who in 1792 received a federal government job, the first mail carrier for Barnstable, told a very strange story. He made his round trip from Boston, bringing the mail back to the village. Many people thought that his position was a government scandal, paying John a very extravagant wage of one dollar a day for making this mail run.

One day, John crossed the path of Samuel Savage. He was looking as strange as ever. John thought that he would be polite to the old man and bid him a good day.

"Hello Samuel! How is the family and the wife?"
"Fine John! Are you still running the mail?" Samuel asked.
"Oh yes! The job is a very good one. How do you like my gray horse?" John tactfully asked.

"Why let me tell you my boy!" Samuel shot back.

"And I looked, and behold a pale horse; and his name that sat on him was death; and hell followed with him." Samuel proclaimed.

Both men stood there silent for several seconds before John Thacher got enough nerve to reply, but Samuel quickly continued;

"Good day!"

Samuel Savage then turned and walked away leaving poor John Thacher speechless.

The strange verse was quoted from the Book of Revelation, but why did Samuel suddenly shout it out? Was it because he was so unhappy with John Thacher's lucrative position; or was it Samuel's family tragedies finally manifesting it; or was he conversing with the spirit world? Maybe, he just went crazy for those few minutes. Know one knows for sure.

Samuel Savage's actions were not just one case. The following account recorded in 1890 tells the same kind of character of this very interesting man who lived at The Barnstable House.

Not too far down the King's Highway lays a large rock alongside the road, just by Henry F. Loring's place in the western part of the village. Our dear Doctor Savage saw this fancy perch of a rock as an opportunity. Like an old crow, he sat upon it nearly everyday, watching for the Cape Cod Stagecoach to round the bend heading into the village, bringing new visitors to Barnstable. As soon as they were within sight, and sound, Samuel would leap to his feet and in his own peculiar manner, and in sepulchral tones, he would announce that he was the physician and surgeon of the Town of Barnstable. (The rock was still there in 1890). The occupants of the stagecoach looked at Doctor Savage in amazement as he stood there yelling out his education from Harvard and his medical credentials to them.

Samuel, though very strange, was indeed very well educated. Between 1783 and 1784, the town of Barnstable did approve a support bill for the poor and allowed Doctor Savage to treat and medicate them, and to bill the town for his services. The town gave him six pounds, eighteen shillings.

Doctor Samuel Savage did in fact contribute to the community with his special abilities in medicine, and personality. He died on 28 June 1831.

A record kept at the Sturgis Library in Barnstable quotes a saying that it claims is on Samuel's gravestone. Edward Yound who was born in 1683, and who died in 1765 wrote it.

It reads;

"Insatiate archer! Could not one suffice?
   Thy shaft flew thrice,
   And thrice my peace was slain."

This author takes this saying as addressing his obvious tragedies throughout Samuel's life. In checking his gravestone at the Cobb Hill Cemetery in 1989, I find no inscription as listed above unless it lies underground.

The stone of Samuel's son John Savage reads:

"Here lies the body of Mr. John Savage, Student of Law son of Samuel and Hope Savage he departed this life

Oct. 5th., 1811 Etatis 22." (At Cobb's Hill Cemetery, Barnstable).

To date, psychic researchers have not established any spirit at The Barnstable House that matches the colorful character of Doctor Samuel Savage.

Dr. Samuel Savage gravestone

Chapter 6

There She Blows !

Chief Justice Lemuel Shaw & Herman Melville

The following account has been partly quoted from "Barnstable, Three Centuries of A Cape Cod Town" by Donald G. Trayser, published by F.B. & F.P. Goss, Hyannis, Massachusetts, 1939. Other inserts are from "Who Were First in The Political Graveyard; and an article from Robert L. Gale.

Lemuel Shaw was born 9 January 1781 at Barnstable. He became a lawyer and was a member of the Massachusetts state house of representatives 1811-14, 1820, 1829; delegate to the Massachusetts state constitutional convention, 1820; member of the state senate, 1821-22; chief justice of Massachusetts supreme judicial court, 1830-60; drew up the first charter of the city of Boston in 1822-23; involved with several major state decisions. He died in Boston 30 March 1861 and is buried at Mt. Auburn Cemetery, Cambridge, Massachusetts.

"Chief Justice of Massachusetts, Lemuel Shaw was a happy man, although, as with everyone, there was sadness, too. Born in Barnstable in 1781 he was educated at home and later at Harvard College where he graduated in 1800. During his first years of studying law at Amherst, he met and courted Nancy Melville, daughter of the venerable Major Thomas Melville of Boston, who later inspired Oliver Wendell Holmes' poem, "The Last Leaf." She was the sister of Allan Melville, Lemuel's friend. Shaw was admitted to the bar in New Hampshire in 1804 but later established at Boston. Shaw's friendship with Nancy resulted in their engagement of marriage, but her untimely death in 1813 cut short their dreams. The saddened youth did not recover from this loss for many years before he bestowed his affections on another. When he was thirty-seven, in 1818, he married Elizabeth Knapp, a wealthy daughter of merchant Josiah Knapp of Boston.

They had two children, John and Elizabeth. Mother Elizabeth died giving birth to her daughter in 1822. Remembering Shaw's early engagement to Nancy Melville, it is interesting to know that his daughter, Elizabeth, in August 1847 married Herman Melville, a grandson of Major Melville.

Lemuel married again around 1827 and becoming very successful was asked in 1830 by Massachusetts Governor Levi Lincoln and also by Daniel Webster to become Chief Justice of the Commonwealth. He did so at a great sacrifice of losing his $15,000 to $20,000 a year law salary to accept the $3,500 by the state. He served as judge from 1830 to 1860 just before his death. Shaw's daughter's distinguished husband, Herman Melville, author of "Moby Dick," and one of the literary great men, dedicated his first book "Typee" to the Chief Justice Lemuel Shaw. No doubt that Lemuel supported Herman in the publication of this South Sea epic in 1846.

While staying in Boston, Melville borrowed Shaw's Athenaeum book membership several times. Though Shaw's first marriage was brief for his wife died after four years it was five years later that he wed Hope Savage, daughter of Doctor Samuel Savage of Barnstable. By this marriage he had two sons, Lemuel and Samuel. Mrs. Hope Shaw survived her husband and lived until 1879. The Barnstable House was passed on through these famous families.

Historical events started to take place around the house. Now related to the family, Herman Melville, the famous novelist returned from his long sea voyages and was seeking a quiet and peaceful settlement so he could write his novel. The surroundings were perfect at The Barnstable House. He needed the mariner atmosphere, and the colonial flare of Barnstable to fuel his creativity for "Moby Dick."

It is not known how much influence the house had over Melville during his stay there, but we wonder if he ever encountered any spirits there as he walked about, or studied the bay through an upstairs window. Can the splashing waves or the harpooning into the flesh of the whale be felt upstairs today? Just a few doors down the street located on a shelf at the Sturgis Library are a copy of "Moby Dick."[7]

---

[7] Partly supplied by the works of Robert L. Gale article "Bartleby – Melville's Father-Law." 2002

Chapter 7

The Many Faces & Names of The House

The house fell back into the ownership of the Davis family around 1803 after the estate of Daniel Davis was settled. But suddenly, it changed hands again and went back to the Savage family. William H. and Charles Savage kept the house throughout most of the eighteen hundreds. There is no record of Captain John Gray owning the house as yet, but he did live there after retiring from the sea. It was changed into an Inn and named, "The Captain Gray's Inn."

The Barnstable House carried several other names as well;

The Blue Lantern
The Black Horse Tavern
The Captain Graves Inn

After the nineteen fifty-six disaster of the Andrea Doria which sunk just off the coast of Nantucket, the owners of the house then changed the name to "The Andrea Doria Inn." Later, another named it "The 1716 House" and placed that date up on the center chimney, which can still be seen today. The name "The Barnstable House" came later and is still called that today.

Captain Graves

Another new spirit started to roam the halls of the house and many researchers claim it to be Captain Graves, a grumpy old man who complains constantly. There was a Henry Graves who had a daughter named Esther D. Graves, and she married in 1873 to Orin L. Crowell, a member of the Boston Marine Society. Could this be our Captain Graves or Gray or Grey?

There is one record of a Tempy Grey at the Cobb's Hill Cemetery in Barnstable. Her stone reads:

> "In memory of Mrs. Tempy Gray wife of Mr. Samuel Gray who departed this life Oct. 10th. 1806 in the 28th. year of her life."

Could this be a relation?

Davis House

From book notes on Old Houses in Barnstable by Francis William Sprague gives the following description of the Barnstable House as being the Davis House:

Davis House, next west of Mr. Fitzgerald's house was built by Mr. Paine (date on chimney). Later the house was owned by Captain Savage. (See Park's History of the

Savage Family). John Gray once lived in this house; now owned by the heirs of Adolphus Davis, a Boston ship owner."

Adolphus Davis

Boston also had a lot of influence on the house. Besides tourists and travelers staying at the house, Bostonian's spent many months living there too. Some escaping the city hustle bustle, others, the hot humid summer of the concrete and wooden buildings. Many were fascinated in the house and bought it. Once owned by the heirs of the Adolphus Davis family, their Boston ship building business brought much high society Bostonian's down to the Cape, sometimes spending weeks at the house.

Paul M. & Gladys Swift

By the time the nineteen twenties rolled in, the rich and famous threw big parties at the house, filled with illegal booze. In 1926, Paul M. and Gladys Swift occupied the home, but soon after it changed hands again. Long term ownership began to fad and one wonders why this occurred?

Thomas Otis

Thomas Otis owned it from 1926 to 1927. He created the Blue Tavern Corporation, and renamed the house "The

Blue Tavern," but sadly to say, his business went into ruin and he had to file for bankruptcy.

Harold A. & Ethelp Daggett

In 1927, Harold A. and Ethelp Daggett took over the place, but it was only in the capacity of administrators. Then, Adolphus Davis took it back.

Governor of Massachusetts

From 1927 to the mid-1930's, the Governor of Massachusetts once lived here at the house. Meanwhile, the population of spirits started to increase according to many visitors who stay there. It was said that the additional ghosts were past tourists who loved it at the Barnstable House and chose to come back there. Many of the ghosts cannot be identified because they come and go so quickly, as if they were still vacationing at the house.

Elmer E. Clapp

Sometime after the bankruptcy of the unfortunate Thomas Otis, Elmer E. Clapp bought the house from an auction. He owned it until 1945 and not much was reported at that time.

Clarence & Mabel Whipple Bangs

After 1945, Clarence and Mabel Whipple Bangs lived at the house until 1949. Again, nothing was reported during these years.

Lucia Neilson

After 1949, Lucia Neilson, the Bacardi Rum heiress bought the place and gave it its first recorded face lift installing modern fixtures, including updating all the fireplaces in the house. An east wing was added which increased the size to several more rooms. The home was now a glamorous mansion of its time. Stories of the spirits there started to surface and suddenly other old Barnstable homes reported having haunting too. The existence of ghost was being more recognized in the community as other did ancient colonial homes devoured its people and history.

Ray H. Orde

Ray H. Orde took over ownership of The Barnstable House from 1953 to 1955.

Linnea K. Svenson

Linnea K. Svenson bought it in 1955 and owned it until 1964. It was updated once again and after the construction settled down Linnea enjoyed the company of the spirits wandering about.

Jack J. Furman

Jack J. Furman owned the house in 1971.

Hans Holzer & Sybil Leek

Tales of Cape Cod, Inc. published a book on "Along Barnstable Village's Historic Mile by Patricia Anderson, Marion Vuilleumier and Jack Frost in 1985. It states the following about the Barnstable House:

"In the 1970's one owner heard of legends that the house was haunted. Inquiries revealed that ghost chaser Hans Holzer and medium Sybil Leek investigated at a lawyer's request and found some indication of ghostly activity. The owner noted she too had felt a friendly presence and had several unexplained occurrences during her tenure."

"But what is a town without at least one house whose former tenants linger around the home they loved so dearly in life!"

Janet G. Johnson

From 1971 to 1974, Janet G. Johnson bought the house and the restaurant, which was made out of the new wing that Lucia Nielson added on after 1949.

John G. Fitzgerald

On 31 Dec. 1984, Mr. Fitzgerald "doing business as" Barnstable House, applied and received from the Commonwealth of Massachusetts and the Town of Barnstable a common victualler's license to be used in conjunction with a food service permit. The cost was $50 and it would expire on 31 Dec. 1985.

Eugene Curry, Esq.

It is not known as of this writing that Attorney Curry is an owner of the building, but his offices of Eugene R. Curry and Associates occupy the Barnstable at 3010 Main Street (Route 6A) in Barnstable from the 1990's to present (Dec. 2002).

Tangerine Inc.

Also, this high tech company occupies part of the house as of 2002. Formed in the summer of 2001, this softswitch manufacturer hopes to succeed in communications. They also take pride in the reputation of the house by stating in their ads that "the Barnstable House previous tenants included Herman Melville and the rumored home of eleven ghosts."

Chapter 8

First Hand Accounts

During the ownership of Janet Johnson between 1971 and 1974, the house and restaurant began to report ghost sightings. The activity of the spirits was very high, and at times Janet was concerned after sinking a lot of money into remodeling it. She added new floors on top the old ones. Walls were torn down or replaced with others. Fireplaces were sealed up in some rooms and new heating systems were installed along with new lighting. All this new construction made the ghost very unsettled. Construction workers and employees were starting to spread stories of ghost throughout the village. Some of murder and personal tragedies, and others strange and even humorous. Many had a witty twist to them.

Janet claims to have never experienced anything herself, but she believed they existed in the house, like little Lucy. She never really knew her name at that time, but she was quoted as saying; "Yes, I do think some unworldly creatures live here," she once said during a newspaper interview.

The following encounters are true accounts reported by various individuals about the spiritual occupants of The Barnstable House.

Encounter #1

One quiet and overcast day, a waitress went about her regular duties of serving customers when the Barnstable House contained a restaurant in it. Taking orders and running back and forth to the kitchen, one customer stopped and asked her for her check. The waitress replied and went off to her counter area to add it up for the lady. As she stood there calculating the figures, the waitress suddenly felt a pair of hands wrap around her, embracing her very tightly.

She twisted around to see who was so bold and found no one there! Suddenly, her blood drained from her head and before she could scream out, the entire room started to spin and fade away until she fell to the dinning room floor, fainting! Customers jumped up and ran over to her rescue. An ambulance was called and she was quickly transported to the Cape Cod Hospital in Hyannis where she told her startling story. After her release, she felt embarrassed; thinking that no one believed her!

Appetizers

New England Clam Chowder	1.25	Cranberry Shrub	.95
Crock of Onion Soup au gratin	2.50	Stuffed Mushrooms	3.25
Soup of the day	.95	Marinated Herring	2.95
Shrimp Cocktail	4.50	Clams Casino	3.75
Fresh Fruit Cocktail	1.50	Clams on the half shell	3.50

Entrees

BARNSTABLE HOUSE SPECIALTY
Roast Prime Rib of Beef au jus
HEAVY WESTERN BEEF
Captain's Cut .. 12.95   Mate's Cut .. 10.95

BONELESS NEW YORK SIRLOIN
BROILED TO YOUR TASTE, CROWNED WITH MUSHROOM CAPS. A GENEROUS STEAK

FILET MIGNON
BROILED TO A TURN. SERVED WITH BEARNAISE SAUCE, BUTTERFLIED UPON REQUEST

SURF 'N' TURF
THE CLASSIC MARRIAGE OF BONELESS SIRLOIN STEAK AND JUMBO SHRIMP

STUFFED FILET OF SOLE
DELIGHT SOLE FILETS STUFFED WITH SHERRIED CRAB AND CRUMB DRESSING SERVED WITH SAUCE NEWBURG

SHRIMP SCAMPI
FOUR LARGE GULF SHRIMP SAUTEED IN HEATED LEMON BUTTER WITH GARLIC

BAKED STUFFED SHRIMP
FOUR LARGE PRAWNS SERVED WITH CHEF'S SPECIAL STUFFING

BAKED OR BROILED SCALLOPS
WITH A LIGHT BUTTER CRUMB TOPPING

BROILED SWORDFISH
A TRUE GIFT FROM THE SEA

SEAFOOD CASSEROLE 9.95
SHRIMP, SCALLOPS, CRAB MEAT, SWORDFISH SERVED IN A VELVETY CREAM SAUCE

Page one of an original menu

CATCH OF THE DAY . . . .
   CHEF'S CHOICE OF FRESH LOCAL SEAFOOD EITHER BAKED OR BROILED
CHICKEN BREAST EUGENIE . . . .
   BONELESS BREAST OF CHICKEN ON HAM AND TOAST POINTS, TOPPED WITH SUPREME SAUCE AND MUSHROOMS
VEAL SCALLOPINI . . . .
   TENDER YOUNG VEAL SAUTEED IN GARLIC AND WHITE WINE SAUCE
ROAST DUCKLING A L'ORANGE 9.95
   DELIGHTFULLY CRISP, WITH A LIGHT SAUCE FLAMBÉ

LOBSTER AMERICANA
Cracked chunks of lobster stewed with vegetables and herbed wine
13.95

All entrees include a crock of cheese and crackers
chilled salad served continental style, chef's vegetables also
served continental style, choice of potato or rice pilaf,
homemade bread.

LIGHT ENTREE
Soup, Salad, Rolls
4.95

FOR CHILDREN UNDER TWELVE
Roast Beef 4.95
Fish · Baked or Broiled 3.95
Chicken 3.95

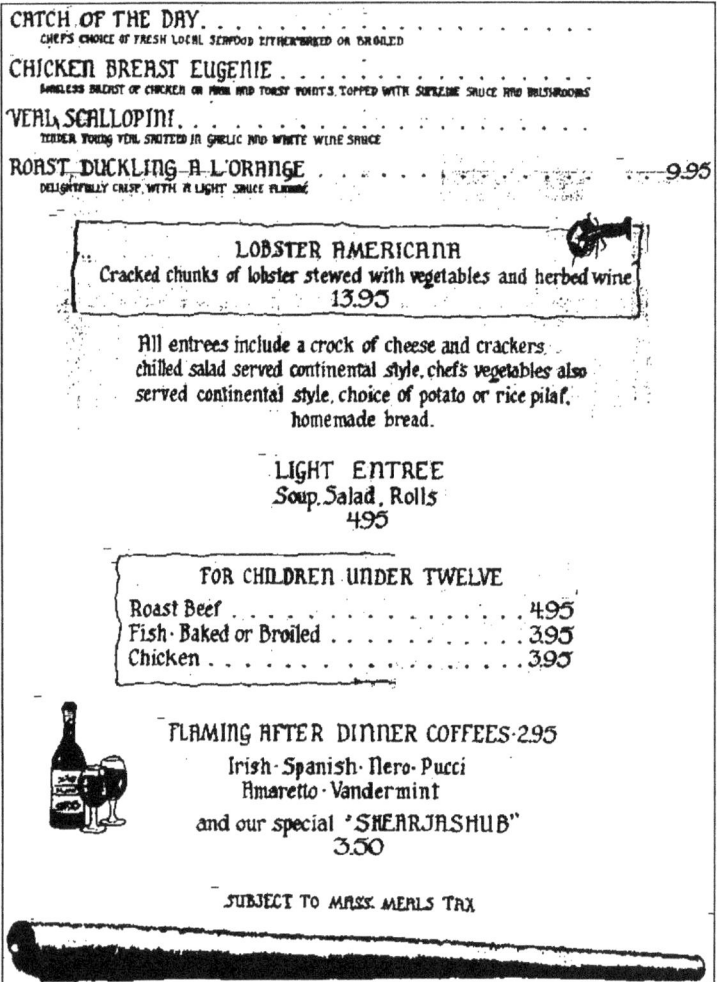

FLAMING AFTER DINNER COFFEES 2.95
Irish · Spanish · Nero · Pucci
Amaretto · Vandermint
and our special 'SHEARJASHUB"
3.50

SUBJECT TO MASS. MEALS TAX

Page two of an original menu

Encounter #2

On a cold dreary night, another employee of the house walked down the stairs and stopped near the foot, just by one of the fireplaces. Suddenly, feeling very strange, he looked about the room thinking that someone else was nearby, standing very close to him. Finding no one, he slowly walked over to the front of the fireplace. Once again, he looked around. To his horror, he was suddenly shaken to death by a burst of flames exploding from the fireplace. The flash of fire frightened him so much that he ran from the room looking for help, and of course, a friendly living person.

Encounter #3

A couple of employee's entered one of the large rooms and found all the candles in the chandelier lit. Puzzled, they both put them all out and started to leave the room. One by one, each candle came back to life in a full glory of vibrancy. Both employee's slowly looked at each other in shock. Getting enough nerve, they re-entered the room and cautiously approached the chandelier. Looking at each other once, they both reached out at the same time and started to put each flame out again. When they stood back, the chandelier illuminated once again. Much braver now, both girls were determined to put that light out. The spirits would win this battle because after several attempts, they gave up and the girls left the room leaving the chandelier in its ghostly glow.

Encounter #4

The employee's always enjoyed serving the winter customers. They were usually the year round residence and the atmosphere was more pleasant and less hectic. Each employee felt warm and comfortable serving their friends and family from the community. The appreciation from the village people was non-hostile and no one was rushed about.

One day, a cheerful waitress arrived at the table of some Cape Codder's and took their orders. She went into the kitchen to pace the orders with the cook. Both customers were talking about how tasty a bowl of New England Clam Chowder would be as they discussed their personal business.

As time went by, they noticed the other waitresses rushing about tending to their customers. The place was packed and full of hungry patrons. Soon, the two elderly ladies noticed that their waitress did not return from the kitchen with their meal. After a few minutes longer, they stopped one of the other waitresses passing by, and asked to have their waitress.
The kind employee acknowledged their request and walked over to another waitress and gave her the message.

The waitress quickly ran over to the hungry ladies and apologized for being so far behind, and explained the instant rush put them behind slightly. She lifted her note pad and pencil and asked the two for their order. Both puzzled ladies looked at each other and said that they already placed their order with another waitress and that she went into the kitchen quite a long time ago and never came out.

After giving the description of their waitress, no one could be matched. Suddenly realizing the reputation of the Barnstable House, the waitress and both ladies took a startled look at each other, and then glanced over at the kitchen doors!

Encounter #5

Many times, customers would spot one ghost that was named Martha from some unknown source. She was said to be a sad bride. Patrons would find her standing in a corner of the dinning room wearing her pretty long wedding dress. Sometimes it appeared white in color, other times blue. She was not a mortal, they said.

Encounter #6

Other spirits would come downstairs and actually sit with customers, talking with them, and even drinking their drinks, gulping them down causing some customers to complain to the management. When a complaint appeared to be authentic, and the waitress knew that they were telling the truth, she would give them another drink and explain that they were just visited by their resident ghost. This practice did not always assure a return trip on the part of the customer!

Encounter #7

The most sensational story came from the 1973 encounter with the Barnstable Fire Department regarding the ghost of Martha. Chief William Jones responded to a call to put out a fire at the Barnstable House. The first engine pulled into the driveway, three firemen jumped off their truck and looked around the grounds. Suddenly, one fireman looked up to the third story window and spotted a lady standing there dressed in a wedding gown looking down at him.

"Do you need any help?" the fireman yelled out. Just then, Chief Jones pulled in with another fire engine. He quickly jumped out and ran over to the front door. Experienced told him not to mess around with these older houses in town. They go up in flames too fast. Upon opening the door, he discovered smoke, so he ran over to the main fireplace and closed the damper. It was midnight and no one was downstairs to greet him, which seemed peculiar.

The fireman who saw the lady upstairs approached the fire chief and asked if she came downstairs yet. Now realizing that someone was in the house, they ran upstairs to investigate. As the chief looked around for the girl, he thought of some stories he had heard about the Barnstable House. The ones about a lady dressed in a gown that was murdered on the third floor.

Discovering so many rooms upstairs, he decided to yell out; "Is they're anyone up here?" Just then, two men came out of one room and asked what was the problem? They had no idea there was even a call made to the fire department about a fire at the house. When asked, they also told the firemen that no lady lived there on the third floor. In fact, not in the entire house! Not convinced, the firemen insisted on searching every room, especially the room where she was spotted. No one was found. Now puzzled, they looked at each other for a few seconds in silence.

After securing the area, the firemen picked up their gear and loaded it on the truck knowing damn well that they saw the lady in the wedding gown. The chief knew it was the spirit he heard of before. Through the years the episode became the fascination with the general public, brining more interest to the house and its ghost who live there. Later, it became a yearly tradition to write ghost stories about the house in the newspapers, usually around the Halloween season.

Encounter #8

Another report from the fire station went like this; Four firemen responded to a call to the Barnstable House. As they arrived, smoke was seen pouring out of a skylight on the roof. All four rushed upstairs to the third floor. One door was nailed shut which puzzled them. With several violent thrusts the door gave way shattering the room silence. The loud vibrations shot throughout the house. There was a small fire found there, which was extinguished immediately. One fireman reached for the skylight window, pulling it shut, while still looking around the room for the source of the fire.

Suddenly, they picked up a very strange feeling and became slightly spooked. The house became very still. Just then, the other fire truck pulled into the parking lot below. One officer ran over to the window, breaking the spell and yelled to the others who just arrived; "Everything is under control!"… Was it?

Back downstairs, the men loaded their trucks and cleaned up. As they stood there, they started to compare their feelings. Suddenly, from behind then, a lady appeared from no where and asked;

"Where are the Dalmatians?"

Thinking that she was a neighbor, one fireman turned around and answered;

"Oh! We don't have one, but it's not a bad idea," he said as he was surprised to find the lady standing there in a wedding gown.

The officer was stunned be the sight. The others look at her with great interests. She just stood there watching them clean up as they returned to their work. Quickly finishing, they turned to address the strange lady again, but she had disappeared as fast as she materialized before them.

Now realizing that she had vanished, one fireman went over to another fire truck and asked the others if they saw the lady dressed in the wedding gown. "MARTHA!" Another fireman called out her name into the night. This would be a night they all would never forget. The Barnstable Fire Department was visited by one of the resident ghosts!

Encounter #9

A previous owner invited some high school students over to spend the night in the Barnstable House for a special school project they were assigned too. The study; "unexplained phenomenon." Like many assignments of this kind, the students were sure it would turn into a bust, or would it?

That night, the owner gave instructions not to make any loud noises and he went quickly upstairs to bed for the night. After a short search for ghost, the students started to giggle and play the radio, which without their knowledge awakened the spirits of the house.

Some researchers say that the spirits that do occupy the Barnstable House are shy, and never bother the living residence, but the noises created by the students demanded some immediate attention so the quiet colonial settling could return to a peaceful slumber mood.

The students had no intention of going to sleep. This was a sleep over, and only mischief would be the result in this event. Upstairs, one or more of the ghosts got aggravated and decided to enter the owner's bedroom. Many spirits travel about a house by way of the old crystal doorknobs.

Deciding to get his attention, the ghosts made their move. Through his pink closed eyelids, the owner saw a bright light. He slowly opened them and noticed a brilliant yellow flickering all over the room. He suddenly sat up and discovered his fireplace ablaze. Frozen there for a few seconds, he finally reached a conclusion and shot out of bed, past the fireplace and races downstairs to where the students were bashing about. He commanded them to stop immediately and get to bed or he would send them home.

The owner races back up to his bedroom to extinguish the fireplace. He grabbed the poker and began to spread the ashes about. Still half asleep, he takes a closer look at what he is doing and finds cold ashes. There is no fire, and the ashes are cold!

Now, wide eyed, the owner slowly turns and looks around his room. He backs up to his bed and crawls under the covers, never taking his eyes off the walls of his bedroom. He pulls his blankets up to his chin and continues his glare. The realization of his resident ghost had finally taken hold of his imagination. If any one of us could see those spirits right now, they probably would have a look of satisfaction across their face.
Downstairs, the students were fast asleep! The owner received the full effect of their homework!

Encounter #10

Another report on the Barnstable House was a fire in every room with smoke pouring out from every level, but when investigated, there were no fires, and no smoke. Upon checking for who sounded the alarm, no one knew who called it in. Over time, the Barnstable Fire Department had their fill of calls to this house.

Chapter 9

Host For Eleven Ghost

(The Encounters Continue)

By 1980, the house was sold again. This time to Richard Lindstedt of Sandwich and once again it was remolded. Richard wanted to keep the tradition of the Inn so the bar was expanded to the back of the building. The Tories of the house were now spreading throughout New England. Knowing these stories, Richard thought that its reputation would attract business, especially after a hole was drilled through the floor in the lobby entry way for all to see the famous "Well" in the cellar, the Well where little Lucy plunged to her death. Only a foot square, a small light bulb hung half way down to illuminates the haunted shaft, giving it an eerie atmosphere.

Story #1

One afternoon when alone in the bar, Richard was cleaning up when suddenly he heard some pots and pans rattling about in the kitchen. It was as if someone was getting ready to prepare the upcoming meals for the day. He decided to investigate, barging into the kitchen expecting to find an early employee. He was shocked to find no one! At that very moment, he realized that his restaurant was truly haunted. The ghost living there never gave him any real cause for fear, except for the first initial introduction to them.

After many years of study, it was discovered that the spirits living in the Barnstable House always disappeared when any construction was going on. It was determined that all the activity, destruction and construction frightened them off until things settled back down to the original peaceful setting. After this period of rebuilding was over, things started to happen again!

Story #2
On a cloudy morning, a waitress decided to go into work early to set up her tables. The cook was already in the kitchen when she arrived and after a few words they both parted and went to their chores. The waitress entered the large dinning room and started filling salt and pepper shakers, washing ash trays when suddenly, she started to get a funny feeling that someone was in the room with her.

She convinced herself into a scary pause, and decided to seek out the cook in the kitchen, hoping maybe he was just playing some cruel joke on her. He was standing in front of his stove preparing the Sunday brunch. Scratching her head, she returned to the spooky dinning room. She tried to return to her duties.

Outside, there was a heavy down pour of rain, but suddenly inside the Inn, it became very still. When the waitress tried to continue her work she suddenly felt a tap on her shoulder. At first, she did not turn around, but did after several more taps pounded away on her shoulder. As she half turned to see who was there, the thought started to enter her mind, but hoping it was not true. Wanting so much to see a silly grin on the face of the cook, instead she found no one there!

The kitchen door was nearly twenty feet away. No way could the cook return in there without her seeing him or the moving doors. Her fear turned into panic as she looked around the dinning room. A ghost tried to get her attention or was playing toying with her emotions, something it successfully did!

Story #3
Richard came in one snowy morning, turned on the heaters and started to make the Inn comfortable for the customers who would soon arrive. He took a short coffee break and sat at one of the tables in the dinning room just across from the main lobby hallway that lead to the front door.

As he began to sip his hot brew, the front door suddenly opened, letting in a gust of snow. He looked down the hallway and saw no one there, but just then, the door slammed shut! Before he could raise to investigate, the door opened once more, then closed again, just enough for someone, or something to enter! Richard walked over and found nothing wrong with the door. Now puzzled, he walked back to his table and sat there watching the door. As he sat there, it continued to open and close at will!

Story #4

On another bad weather day, Richard stayed overnight with his faithful dog. It was a very rainy evening; he had a lot of paperwork to complete in his office up on the second floor. As he sat there working on some reports, his dog got up and wandered about the office, then down the hall to the opposite side of the house.

He started to sniff around. One of the spirits was close by. Suddenly aware it, the large hound became frightened and started to back up. He barked loud, and then howled at a door where the ghost was entering. Richard got up to investigate and found his dog shaking to death locked inside a room. He was very puzzled over how the dog got locked up in the room. The poor thing never displayed such fear over anything. He had badly scratched the wall near the door as if in desperation to get out.

Richard was now frightened himself. He looked around the room and down the dark hallway, once a friendly space. The rain battered the roof just one floor above him. His mind started to fill with spooky thoughts and images. Not able to stand it any longer, the dog took off down the hall and down the stairs, with Richard not far behind him.

Story #5

This was the last straw! Richard decided to look up the best spirit researchers in the field. He started right at the top of the list with an invitation to Hans Holzer, and the famous medium, Sybil Leek. The day they stepped into the

Barnstable House was an exciting one. The air was filled with psychic energy as they walked slowly through its halls.

It didn't take them long to discover that there was at least eleven spirits occupying the house at that time. They found that the lady living on the third floor was named Martha and that she was quite beautiful. Hans and Sybil determined that she lived during the colonial period. Their findings gave great credibility to all the stories of the past.

This fascinated Richard very much so he decided to let other researchers into the house, some with infrared equipment, special cameras and tape recorders hoping to gather more evidence on the many ghost who lived there. It wasn't long before the first seance was conducted too.

Each finding showed that there was more than one spirit living in the house, plus many agreed that the number was eleven. They felt that a sea captain and Martha were living upstairs with little Lucy.

Discovering eleven crystal doorknobs proved the avenue they all traveled through because these old doorknobs were pure enough to form a channel from the past and other worlds according to psychics.

Story #6
An unnamed employee heard footsteps one night as she cleaned her work area. They were coming from the next floor above. She knew there was no one in the house, and after checking it out, this proved her correct. Her find made

her very concerned. The following few minutes got very spooky and the house became very eerie, to the point of her running out of the Inn in fear.

Story #7

One night, a white ghostly figure floated right by an employee with no warning or noise. She could see right through the spirit as it glided past her. The poor girl darted off in the opposite direction.

Story #8

Another case was reported involving a waitress who was changing her clothes upstairs. As she got into her work uniform, she suddenly got the feeling that someone, or something was in there with her. She held her breath and slowly looked about in fear. Her feeling would not go away. Carefully, she reached for the door and grabbed the crystal knob. One quick turn and pull, it opened and she was free to run in fear for her life!

Story #9

The phone always rang with no one at the other end. This was always annoying. Richard Lindstedt said that many nights became tense as the house came to life. Many spirits appeared and moved about. They always felt safe after the busy daytime life of the mortals was over. The spirits never threatened Richard and they appeared very friendly to him. The feeling of suspense was still in each room as they roamed about.

Chapter 10

1983 To 1985

(There's More)

Report #1

At 2 Am one early morning, Dereck Lorrigon, a former employee and resident of the Barnstable House was sleeping upstairs in his room when suddenly he was awakened by a piano playing downstairs. Wiping his eyes clear, and trying to focus them on something in his room, he thought he was dreaming at first over the music he was hearing. As it continued to play, Dereck knew he was really awake. He got out of bed and went downstairs to investigate. The piano was positioned in the large dinning room and was within sight as he walked through the main hallway heading for it. He stepped over the small floor window looking down at the Well in the cellar, and took a look around.

Now focusing on the piano in the other room, he discovers a lady sitting on the bench. She had a beautiful blue gown. Somehow this lady didn't appear real. In fact, Dereck could see through her. Now frightened, he took a closer look, and she disappeared in front of him. He stood there shocked for a few seconds, and then decided to check the entire area hoping to find her. His conclusion of a ghost left him standing all-alone in shock in the middle of the dinning room.

Report #2

On another occasion, Dereck and his friend, David Linsted (Lindstedt) who was the son of Richard were climbing the stairs heading for the third floor. When they reached the top, all the doors suddenly slammed shut!

They cautiously entered their room and five minutes later, the slamming repeated. They both shot out of the room and ran down the hall hoping to find the joker. Before their eyes, all the doors suddenly closed again. They opened one door, but it slammed shut, right in their face.

They desperately tried to open it, but it would only crack open six inches, as if someone on the other side was holding it. After several attempts, it finally gave way to a cold and empty room. They investigated every room and found nothing. The strange happening was gone! The spirits stopped their game!

Report #3

A man named Michael Cox was building a comfortable fire in the front hallway fireplace when he heard footsteps on the second floor. The steps were coming in his direction! He turned to see who it was and before his eyes he found a pair of ankles belonging to a woman. Attached to the ankles was a long veil and train from her gown. There was nothing in between! There was no face or hands, but it was concluded that it was Martha who didn't quite materialize before Michael.

This sighting got Michael interested in the haunting of the house and he and his friend decided to set up a tape recorder and two microphones to capture sounds of the spirits. They hung one over the staircase and placed the other at the end of the hallway. They attached two headphones to themselves and went downstairs to wait out any results coming from the bugged third floor above. The wait wasn't long!

Suddenly, a voice cried out in a whispering tone.

"Where is Mary Ellen?" the voice said from upstairs.

Both men turned and looked at each other in total shock! They had just heard the voice of a real ghost!

Report #4

In June 1985, workmen were called in to do some small repairs at the back of the house. As they started to work they began to hear doors swinging back and forth. Upon investigating, they saw the two kitchen doors suddenly burst open in the opposite direction, going against the hinges. They were bent completely around. They checked the entire area and found no one there to take claim to the damaged doors.

During other occasions many people wanted to experience the ghost by spending the night at the house. They only appeared to those that did not expect their visits. It was their game and their rules. Many curious people left empty handed.

As of June 1985, the house was still open for business as "The Barnstable House," a restaurant that seated one hundred and seventy-five customers, a bar that catered to the night crowd of the village, and a few rooms to rent upstairs. Of course, only to the brave soul who dared spend a night there?

The present owner was now eager to place the house up for sale. The doors finally closed after July of that same year.

After standing vacant a short time. The unoccupied house was stricken by water damage and decay started to take it toll. Careless people left windows open, and weeds grew high around the grounds. The once beautiful white picket fence fell into ruin, and without running a dehumidifier. The small stream in the cellar slowly turned the basement into a moldy, musty chamber of rot.

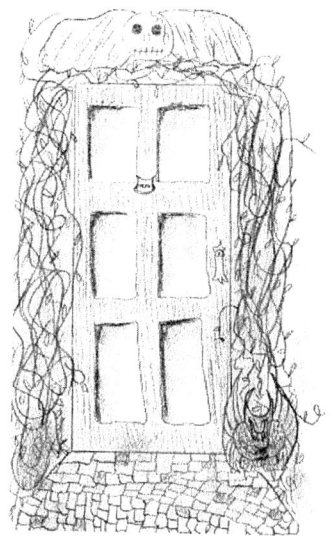

The Door !

Chapter 11

Who Yah Gonna Call !

30 October 1985, 7:30 PM

(The Day Before Halloween)

A special deal was negotiated before the sale of The Barnstable House went through. Radio Station W.B.V.F., on dial 105.7 from Boston wanted to air one of their shows from the house. This was not like any other radio show because it was to be scheduled on 30 October 1985, one day before Halloween. Wanting to broadcast a program from a famous haunted house, they hired a psychic to also come in and search for any ghost!

"This is the new W.V.B.F. station on your 105.7 radio dial from Boston, but tonight we are broadcasting from the Barnstable House here on Cape Cod. Listener's, this is the Wallie and Lauren show and later on we will have a real live medium that will try to contact some of the ghosts that live here at The Barnstable House. Stay tune and join us as we explore the mysteries that are hidden within these walls."

Lauren played more songs for the listener's from the small sitting room just inside a side entrance door to the house, which was used for many years as the main entrance. Speakers were placed all throughout the house blasting out Rock'n'Roll music. This was a new sound to the ghosts, and it sent them hiding in every closet and far away corner of the house upstairs.

The house was torn up from disrepair and various construction projects gone badly. The disc jockeys had invited many guests besides the medium and her two friends. Upon entering, everyone had to sign a release form stating that the radio station and owners of the house were not responsible for anything that might happened to them during their visit.

The house was set up for the public likes never before. Its past two hundred years of colonial life was now being shattered by modern Rock music.

The popular song, "Ghost Busters," rang out in every room through the large speakers as the disc jockeys played it for their audience. Tomorrow was Halloween, and the atmosphere was just right for a haunting as a bright full moon lit up the chilly thirty-nine degree night outside.

People started to arrive with the help from the continued broadcasting. Many of them appeared strange and weird. Some thought they were mediums, and others thought they were the ghouls and spirits of the night. Others were just curious and nosy.

The big show was about to begin as a lone red van pulled up into the driveway. Three people get out and walk up to the side door and knock. As the door opens, the disc jockey replays the "Ghost Buster" theme.

"Who yah gonna call! Ghost Busters!" blasted out over the speakers.

All three visitors stood there shocked at the circus going on inside this historical landmark. They slowly looked at each other in doubt of being there. Suddenly, a strange young girl dressed in black appeared out of nowhere wearing a black cape. She floated past them!

"Good evening!" she said in a spooky tone, and then drifted into another room.

A tall man and his son wandered about the hallway peeking into every dark corner hoping to spot a spirit. A thin ghostly looking character slowly walked up to the door and greeted the psychic and her two friends.

"Are you the ones?" he asked in a mysterious manner, but quickly left before getting an answer.

The medium and her two students took another look around and thought seriously about leaving the carnival behind. But something told them to step inside and shut the door behind them. Walking into the small room to their right, the psychic introduced herself and her friends.

"Hello! I am Donna Miller, your medium, and these are my friends, Leslie and Paul."

Lauren was manning the microphone and took advantage of her entrance. He announced that the medium was there and that contact with the spirits would soon begin. Wallie took all three down the hallway to show them around the entire downstairs area. He asked Donna what she would need and she answered;

"Nothing really. Just show us the way to upstairs."

Her feelings were telling her to go upstairs and as they walked towards them they noticed each room containing lit candles. The house appeared so spooky and the strangers wandering about kept popping out of every closet and corner. The lack of heating created an eerie atmosphere and one would have trouble telling the difference between a visitor and a ghost. On the second floor they came across the same young lady dressed in black. This babe was off her rocker as she mumbled words softly to herself, drifting just a few feet behind them.

Donna suddenly sensed a strong energy coming from each room, but the back room facing the Cape Cod Bay attracted her the most.

"There are many spirits in here and much has happened here throughout the years."

The room was very dark and still. One of Donna's friends turned slightly and jumped nearly out of her skin. A tall thin man suddenly appeared from the hidden shadows of the room. He was watching every move the psychics made, getting closer with each step. Wallie joined them as they continued their journey around the second floor. He handed them a couple of flashlights to help in their search. He really showed a lot of genuine interest in Donna's investigation. The theatrics was another thing he had to do for the public interests.

A bedroom located at the front of the house, opposite the parking lot contained little energy, but suddenly one friend of Donna's noticed heavy claw marks just next to the door on the inside wall. Each grove was very deep into the plaster as if something tried to desperately get out of the room. The thing or animal that got caught in this room must have been very frightened at what it saw!

A fireplace was located right in the hallway with a very large mirror over its mantle. One of the friends walked over and inspected the antique fixture and while doing so, he peered into the glass catching a glimpse of the same spooky girl who was still floating about. He turned to his left to see her and she was gone. There, next to him on the mantle was an Ouji board. The eerie sight scared him. He turned to his right and saw the tall thin man staring right at his face from a dark corner nearby. Turning back to the glass mirror, he now saw the man and the strange girl peering at him. Now frightened, he rushed up to catch the other researchers who were just entering another room.

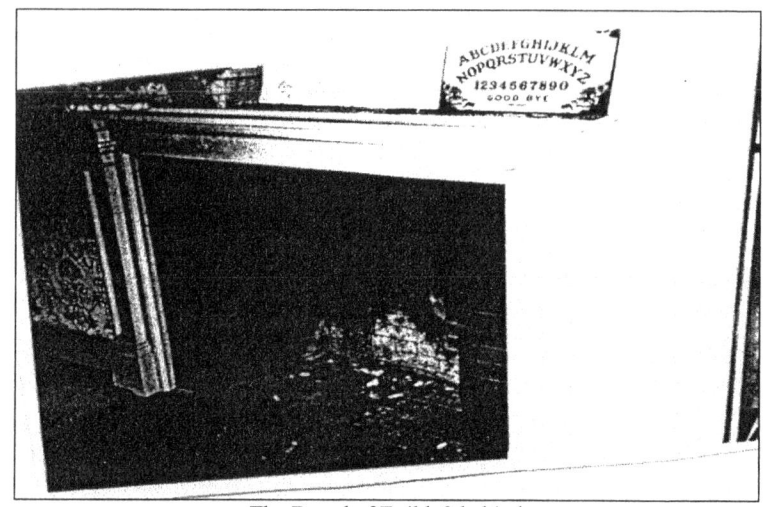
The Board of Evil left behind

The next room faced the side parking lot where a small window once revealed Martha looking down at the firemen. The small panes were clouded over with dirt. A desk stood in the corner giving the purpose of the room away. Several other people joined the medium in her search, hoping to get a look at a real ghost. One strange lady said;

"I've seen the ghost over here. They've talked to me."

The window the bride Martha was seen in by firefighters

The search party looked at each other and left the odd lady behind. They now headed for the third floor where much had been reported in the past. The stairway creaked as several people tried to fit their way up its narrow passage. Now, much colder then the other floors, Donna says there is a presence nearby!

Dark paneling covered the walls and ceiling, even the closets. Much of the hallway had hanging archways, very low where some of the shortest people had trouble passing through. Once inside a small room, everyone gathered around. Containing only a small broken down couch in the center of the room, only a tiny window lit the space from the full moon outside. Many newspapers and trash was lying all over the floor. There were three small closets, which were actually crawl spaces into the eves of the lower part of the roof. Each had home made doors made of plywood. Everyone took notice of the dark inside.

"I feel something here! This is where we will start." Donna instructed.

She and one of her friends sat on the small broken down couch with one other woman. The others all stood around waiting for Donna to make first contact. Eyes traveled about the room. Everyone was scared quiet as they inspected every corner. Wallie was hooked on what was taking place. He took the mike to one side of the room and reported to Lauren who was downstairs playing songs and entertaining the public, waiting for the first report to come in from upstairs.

Suddenly, Donna spoke; "I am going to try to locate a spirit in here."

Everyone turned their eyes to her, waiting for her next move. The room was supper silent!

"I will concentrate on the energy of the room and try to contact any spirit who wishes to come forth."

Donna slowly closed her eyes with her two friends following. The room remained silent. Only the sounds of heavy breathing from a few people and the cold wind outside were heard. An added light with the full moon in the room was donated from a lone street light from across Route 6A outside.

Shadows slowly danced across the walls as people started to sway from there prolong standing. Donna's deep breath told others that she was now in a deep state. The stage was set for one of the most exciting moments of the evening. Quiet reined! Everyone waited for it to happen!

Donna's friend, Paul stood off to one side of the couch watching her search out for spirits. He looked around the room, stopping at one of the small closet doorways. Unable to see inside to the attic, he stared into the dark opening, later turning his attention back to Donna.

Psychic, Donna Miller and friend Leslie in 3rd. floor room

Suddenly, a small flicker of light caught the corner of his eye. He turned back to the closet, peered back into the dark hole, waiting for the light to appear again.

"There it is again," he said to himself.

This time he could make out what it was!

"It was a small figure!"

"A little girl!"

"It was a little girl with ribbons in her hair, a light colored dress and a very playful look in her eyes!"

The crawl space in 3rd. floor room where Lucy played hide and seek

Blinking once or twice, Paul tried to focus his eyes on the figure better, thinking he was wrong in what he saw. He continued to see the little girl peek around the corner at him. He felt that no one would believe him if he declared his image. Her figure was very slight, but it was clearly a little girl. He stood there watching in amazement while she played with him.

"There is a presence!" Donna instructed.

Paul knew she was correct, but he was deathly afraid no one else would see what he was seeing so he kept his mouth shut and continued to stare at her. The others in the room had their eyes focused on Donna. Paul prayed someone else would spot the little girl to confirm his sighting. Then suddenly, it came from a man standing directly across from him. He softly cries out;

"Hey! Do you see that?"
"It's a little girl! A ghost!" he added softly, but very excited.

Everyone looked in shock, bending their necks trying to get a view of the little girl. Paul suddenly got a wide smile across his face. His vision was verified. He continued to keep his eyes on the little spirit. Donna was not facing the closet, but she spoke without turning;

"It is the little girl who lives up here. She has bows in her hair, a light dress and a small ball. She is very playful and is very interested in us."

Donna was great! She hit the nail right on the head without seeing Lucy. Paul acknowledged that he too was watching the little girl all along.

The small girl continued to peek around the corner being extremely quick in her moves, but soon she faded into the darken closet. Donna said that the little girl was seeking someone to play with.

After several attempts to get other spirits to appear, Donna gave up by suddenly leaving the small room. At first moment, everyone was left behind wondering what had happened. Some kooks still hung behind hoping to see more ghosts. Finally, everyone followed Donna downstairs to where Lauren and the radio station were.

Upon arriving there, the listeners were getting on ear full from Lauren's reports. He then pushed the mike into Donna's face forcing her to tell her side of the story. After that, they headed back upstairs. Now the entire world knew the spirits living in the Barnstable House were friendly and nature loving, but noises did disturb them.

Lauren and Wallie were spending the night in the house as part of the show so they were happy to hear that the spirits were friendly, even though there was still a sound of caution in their voices. The second trip upstairs went in failure so they decided to explore the mysteries of the "Well" and the cellar below the famed window in the floor.

People were still pouring in as the psychic party went down the old wooden stairway, each step cracking on the way down. The cellar floor was still made of earth smelling of dust and mold. Below, everyone shuffled around the

Well. Not much to look at, the stream was now a line of water tinkling by their feet. Almost in unison, all eyes peered upward to the glass window. After that, they looked around the cellar walls, exploring every nook and cranny of the old boards that made them.

Donna concentrated on bringing forth a spirit there. She quickly spoke!

"There is an Indian down here! I'm not sure why he is down here. He just seems to be wandering around."

The reading was very short, not revealing much more about the Indian. They went back upstairs where the music was still blasting and people were now exchanging ghost stories.

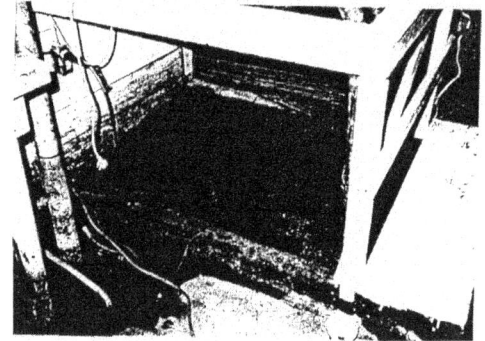

Window in 1ˢᵗ floor looking down into cellar well.
The well fenced in with modern flooring all around.

Chapter 12

Back Upstairs, For More Scares!

On the main floor, the restaurant and bar was abandoned, old and dusty furniture lay scattered about. It appeared very spooky, as if the owners had left without taking anything with them. The staircases were old and shaky, and outside, it was pitch black, giving the effect of a real haunted house, which of course, it was! The researchers returned upstairs to investigate further.

The first room they entered was about sixteen by twenty feet. It looked like it was used as an apartment. It contained only a closet and bathroom. The flashlights were turned off in case of another sighting. Donna started to call out to the spirits while also answering a question someone asked;

"They can appear as a smoky haze or shadow, or even lights. They can appear in any form."

"Do they come out more during Halloween?" Wallie asked after joining the group.

"A full moon attracts a lot of spirits, but they mostly come out on Halloween because people create that energy, hoping to see them. This is why there are so many reports around this time. We are close to a full moon now and that will also attract them." Donna explained.

The interested disc jockey asked her more questions about the spirits and their habits. Holding the mike in their travels he continued to ask about the "Well" and if it mattered with having the house located over it. Donna said that it did not matter. Speaking into the mike, Wallie said;

"It's ten thirty-nine, and we'll be on the air till midnight."

Hoping to look for cold spots, Donna bounced from one room to the next. This would also tell her if they were present. They entered the room where the fire took place as reported by the firemen in above chapters. Wallie was suddenly frightened from being left behind without a flashlight. His open radio line to listeners and Lauren gave them all a creepy glimpse as to what was happening.

They entered that same room where the little girl was sighted an hour earlier. Donna had seen a man wearing a long dark coat walking around outside the room. He quickly disappeared. Her concentration was not in tune with the room and no spirits were present, so they quietly gave up and went on to another room as the radio audience paused for a commercial. When they came back on the air, Lauren said the following;

"It's forty degrees outside and we are going to have Father Guido Sarducci stooping by. It's ten fifty-one, now cloudy and very cold outside. This is W.B.V.F. radio. I would like to take a few minutes right now and talk to a couple of our guest who have stopped by to see our show," Lauren said.

"Your name sir?"

"Richard Lewis."

"Why did you come by the Barnstable House tonight?" Lauren asked.

"I was hoping to see some spirits," Richard replied.

"This is a marshy area isn't it?" Lauren asked.

"Yes! The harbor adds to the eerie surroundings too," Richard said.

"How did you hear about the stories at the house? Is it true that your children saw some ghost around here as they passed by one night?"

"Yes! But also my wife and her friends saw a ghost. The stories run rampant about this place," Richard said.

Spotting another visitor, Lauren sticks the mike into his face!

"Sir! What is your name, and where are you from? Are you here looking for ghosts?"

"My name is David Morrie, and I', from Yarmouth. I have already found the spirits!" he answers in a strange manner.

Lauren's eyes open widely and he replies;

"OK! We will go back upstairs and see what Wallie is up too."

Upstairs, there was a slight problem with one of the visitors who was following Donna around. Frightened over some past childhood experience, Donna was holding the man's hand, trying to comfort him. The spirits felt that fear in him and they stayed out of the room. Just before this incident, Donna had felt the little girl again, and the presence of Martha who was now in a white brides gown walking about. She would not materialize. Disturbed over all the people around Donna, Martha decided to leave.

Donna reached into her pocket and pulled out a good luck crystal, which she used during her readings to secure a favorable vocal point. She still felt the two spirits nearby as the fearful man finally settled down. Donna assured Wallie that all the spirits in the house were not negative and everyone had nothing to fear by spending the night in the house.

"You mean, we will not be hit with an ax or cut into little pieces while we sleep?" Lauren interrupted as he listened to them over the mike.

"It is 11:12 PM, the Boston Celtics won their game tonight and the Megabucks numbers are, 5, 8, 12, 17, 24, 27. Father Sarducci is now with us." Lauren announced.

"I'm a pick'n up'a good'd vibrations," the comic priest sang out as he entered the room.

"Father! What do you think about the house?" Lauren asked.

"This is a kind'a house you sit around'a and tell'a funny stories. I just'a flew in'a from'a Rome'a," he said in his Italian accent.

"Are your arms tired?" Lauren comically asked.
"Do you have any ghost stories to tell, Father?" he added.

"Once'a time'ma in'na seminary, I heard'a bang in the hallway and I didn't have time'a to put'a on'a thing, so I went'a out'a into the hall to see what'a it'a was. This it was'a ghost'a," he explained.

"Were you scared?" Lauren asked.

"I was'a scared shirtless," he replied.

"Will you be here throughout the night, father?" Lauren asked.

"Yes'a."

"Did you bring anything to protect us from the ghosts?" Lauren asked.

"Yes'a! I bring something to exorcize with." He replied.

"Oh! What is that?" Lauren asked.

"A Jane'a Fonda exorcize tape'a," he answered.

Suddenly, loud noises came from Wallie's mike upstairs; "Scratch! Bang! Scrape! #@!?!."

Jokingly, Wallie was trying to create a spooky scene to scare the listeners. The time was 11:21 PM and the station would soon be off the air at twelve o'clock. The search party made their way downstairs, now standing in front of the large old fireplace in the side sitting room where the show was being aired.

Standing there, warming their cold bodies, one of Donna's friends saw something in the fire. It was a startling message coming right out of the flames, sending a warning! She turned quickly to Donna and asked her to step aside with her.

"Donna! I feel that there is going to be a big fire here tonight if they are not careful. Can you warn them of this? I saw it in the fireplace! I saw a large log roll out onto the floor catching everything on fire while they all sleep," Leslie said.

"Sure thing hun! Don't you worry, I will tell them right now. They'll listen to me," Donna explained.

She took Wallie to one side and explained the vision to him. His expression on his face ran white and cold as he got the message. He nodded his head in agreement and caution would definitely be taken before going to bed.

Lauren had just completed an interview with Richard Linstredt, a previous owner of the house. His haunting story of the sighting of Martha downstairs sent chills through some listeners.

A lone customer entered into one of the recently finished rooms to find the young spirit standing there looking at her. The sight was unbelievable! The patron came running over to Mister Linstedt shouting out that a woman was standing in the next room without any feet. Richard came to the conclusion that Martha was standing on one of the original floors six inches below the new one. After all, physical features mean little to them!

As Lauren began to recap the evening events, the Psychic party went back upstairs to search out spirits one last time before calling it a night. Once on the second floor, the house appeared more spooky as many visitors were now gone. Donna's two friends went on their own to another room. There, they stopped in front of a sealed up fireplace. A small hole was punched into the concealing bricks making it too hard to look down the shaft. The smell of musty, dirty debris gave the two an eerie feeling. One stepped back and bumped into a lone person peering over them suddenly scaring them half to death.

He was a tall thin man dressed in a black overcoat. Appearing out of nowhere, the startled couple could only respond by saying;

"Oh! Excuse me!

Then he said in such a mysterious voice;

"They are in there you know!"

His words sent chills through both their bodies.

"What do you mean?"

"I mean, they hid the bodies in the fireplace, and then covered it up!" the stranger replied.

Stranger in black coat trying to spook us all, then disappears. Was he real?

Now, totally frightened, the two decided to slip away from the weird creature and left the room. Just before leaving, one turned to take a last look at the guy to get a good picture of his face, just in case there were bodies found in there some day. To his surprise, the stranger vanished into thin air!

Downstairs, cots were being laid out for the overnight stay. Lauren began to sign off for the evening;

"Well folks! We are going to sign off and we are sorry to say that Donna, our psychic says that the spirit level is now too low for any ghosts to appear, but she assures us that they are still in many of the rooms. That makes us feel real comfortable as we prepare for bed. Remember! We will be back on the air at 5 AM to give you a full report of our overnight stay. This is W.V.B.F., 105.7 on your dial. Good night!"

Chapter 13

A Bump In The Night

Tired, Lauren and Wallie were actually glad to see the last person leave as they both commented how short the night sleep would be. A man named Ivan Slovan also was spending the night with the two disc jockeys, bunking right next to Wallie. As they lay there, they recapped the entire evening, watching the hypnotic flicker of the flames coming from the fireplace. Soon, the dance of the flames put them all to sleep. The house was now quiet!

After a few hours, the spirits began to dance about, some playfully, others just doing their thing, as they have done for hundreds of years. But, little Lucy had other ideas! Wanting to explore downstairs, she descended to the main hallway, peeked around a corner and found the mortal beings fast asleep. Having a fascination for hair, she slowly drifted over to the slumber party. The adventure was to much to bare, but suddenly she was taken back by Lauren waking up and yelling to the others;

"Wallie! Ivan! Wake up! Look!"

The men jumped to their feet and scrambled about the room like the three stooges. Before their eyes was a large burning log that rolled out of the fireplace coming to rest in the middle of the room starting to set it ablaze. Acting quickly, they recalled the warnings from Donna, to watch out for the fire!

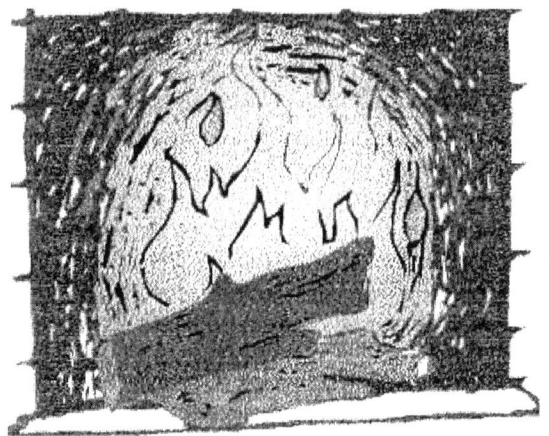

Watch out for the burning logs

As quick as all the excitement started, it ended. The men were too tired and soon fell fast asleep again. Lucy started her adventure once again. The breathing in the room became very heavy assuring the little spirit that they were all out. There she stood, between Ivan and Wallie's head. Now, staring at the wavy hair before here, she tried to get enough nerve to reach for it. Finally, she placed her hand on Ivan's head and ran her little fingers through his hair. He turned about on the cot from the light touch, but that didn't stop Lucy as she continued to message his scalp.

Suddenly, Ivan opened his eyes wide. He felt the sensation running through his hair. Like a rocket, he shot up and off the cot, running his own fingers through his hair.

Pacing around the room did not relieve his strange feeling of the touch of Lucy's small hand. She stood back, peeking around the doorway at the crazed man walking about.

Ivan stopped and looked at his watch. It was nearly airtime so he went into a small room to wake himself up from the nightmare. He couldn't stop running his own fingers through his scalp.

Lucy was still feeling brave so she entered the room once more. She slowly reached out and started running her hand through Wallie's hair until the same thing happened to him. Wallie was now standing next to his cot feeling his scalp and looking around the room. He spotted Ivan in the next room. His smiles across his face made Wallie think that he was the culprit. Ivan knew differently!

"It got you too huh?"

"I don't know about you, but it felt like a little kids fingers running through my hair," Wallie cried out while still running his fingers through his hair in amazement.

After comparing notes, they both came up with Lucy as the one pulling the prank. They were now believers in the science of psychic phenomenon. Today was Halloween, Lauren was up and the 5 AM show was on the air with the headlining story!

Chapter 14

Happy Halloween 1985

"Live! From The Barnstable House, here on the Cape," Lauren announced.

Wallie was in the background dragging heavy objects around and making spooky sounds.

"Today, is October thirty-first, nineteen eighty-five, Halloween day. It is forty-seven degrees outside and last night was a thriller for us, folks. Donna Miller, a medium contacted nine ghosts in the building."

"A little girl around four or five years old[1], dark hair with little white ribbons in her hair. She had blue eyes and was very pretty and happy, and we can all tell you, very playful too."

"A woman in a long Victorian gown, long blond hair piled high on her head. She wasn't very happy with having us all here in the house. She wanted us all to leave."

"There were also two gentlemen living upstairs."

"A captain who was a big burly man with a large beard."

"A farmer who worked for the captain."

"A man in a long dark coat who walked the halls all night."

"A man with a mustache who wore glasses. He also lived upstairs."

"And finally, an Indian who was in the basement. He was the one we read about in the book."

"This is W.V.B.F., 105.7 on your dial, Boston. We are Lauren and Wallie, and what a night we had."

"Wallie, your hair looks a little whiter today. Why is that? Come in Wallie! Where are you?" Lauren called out over the mike.

---

[1] Lucy's age varies with each eye witness or quoted report.

"Woo, Woo! Can you hear me Lauren? I'm upstairs and there are no ghosts today. This room is very cold, which means there should be spirits here," Wallie reports.

"Did you ever stop to think that there is no heat up there?" Lauren Suggests.

"Well folks! Uncle Wallie is upstairs in a room where a captain hung himself," Lauren Said.

"Ah, Lauren! I just experienced a rush of very cold air. I'm not kidding either! Donna said this means spirits were moving about. I'm coming down right away," cried Wallie.

"I must say folks! We have been having a very interesting time here at the Barnstable House. A strange thing happened this morning while we were sleeping. Ivan Slovan, a two hundred and forty pounder, and Wallie fell asleep after making such a racket last night, but were later awakened by the playful hand of the little girl running her fingers through their hair," Lauren told the listeners.

"I couldn't believe it was really happening," Wallie said as he entered the room.

"It lasted for nearly thirty seconds. I really believe it was the little girl. The fingers were so small," he added.

"I think all this that had happened had something to do with the six pack you put away before turning in last night," Lauren said jokingly.

"It was pretty eerie folks and there was no six pack. I would like to thank Donna Miller for coming out last night. It wasn't a séance that you see on TV it was deep concentration on these spirits and a lot of patience in this cold weather," Wallie said.

"Well folks! That raps it up for now! This is W.V.B.F. radio 105.7 on your dial, Boston with Lauren and Wallie, here at the Barnstable House on Cape Cod. It's now forty-six degrees outside and we'll leave you with this great song!"

(The song is already playing softly in the background when Lauren turns it up).

"I ain't afraid of no ghost! Ghost Busters! I ain't afraid of no ghost!"

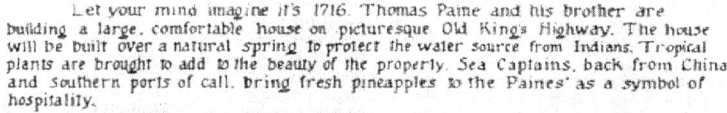

Let your mind imagine it's 1716. Thomas Paine and his brother are building a large, comfortable house on picturesque Old King's Highway. The house will be built over a natural spring to protect the water source from Indians. Tropical plants are brought to add to the beauty of the property. Sea Captains, back from China and southern ports of call, bring fresh pineapples to the Paines' as a symbol of hospitality.

Large rooms are built for family comfort and fireplaces are added for warmth during the long New England winters. The house is built close to the main road for the convenience of the weary traveler on horse back. The home the Paines built will last centuries. You are there now.... The Barnstable House.

In 1716, the home's builders could not have imagined that their house would belong to Doctors, Lawyers, Politicians, and Authors. Dr. Savages granddaughter married Herman Melville. It is believed that he penned the first draft of the American classic "Moby Dick" in the upstairs study, overlooking Barnstable Harbor.

One of the owners of the house, Shearjashub Bourne, promised to 'Return Forever'. We have named our after dinner coffee after him. We hope, if you try our specialty, you too will return again and again.

Relax and enjoy the centuries of heritage in this beautiful home. Once you've dined with us and enjoyed the ambience, we hope you will know why we say "The Barnstable House... a restaurant with spirit."

THANK YOU · · PLEASE COME AGAIN

3010 MAIN STREET, · BARNSTABLE, MASSACHUSETTS 02630

An old advertisement

Chapter 15

Another Session At The House

December 1985

Two months after the great Halloween radio party at the house, Donna, her friend who got us access, and this author and my wife Leslie brought together several friends and family at our home to explore the supernatural. Donna conducted classes and the students were Jackie, Dorothy, Pat, Dorothea employee's who worked with me at Augat, an electronics company, Birget, who was from Germany living with us as an exchange student, Matthew, our son, and Rhonda, our close friend and of course my wife and I.

On one occasion, we got permission once again to visit the Barnstable House to conduct a psychic session there during one of the coldest wintry nights in December. The house was dark and dreary as we all pulled into the driveway. It was a fight to get to the side door entrance because the wind was pushing us back every inch of the way.

Once inside, the temperature was much warmer around thirty degrees. We were all freezing upon entering the side room where the radio show was being aired from. We all brought chairs and placed them in a circle in the middle of the room. Candles and flashlights were all we had to see our way around. We walked about for a short time to get the feel of the house. It was in such a decaying condition. We did manage to get down into the basement to view the popular spring and well there. For some strange reason, the light bulb down there worked the only electricity in the entire house! As we gathered around the spring, it became very still. The only movement down there was the light bulb, which was slowly swinging back and forth. The short moment of silence ended and we all carefully ascended the old narrow stairway.

Donna quickly called our special meeting together so we all seated ourselves in the circle, very close to stay warm. The glow of candlelight created a spiritual atmosphere. Each face glowed with a ghostly white smoky color. We all reached out and held our hands together like a chain. The room suddenly went still. All we could hear was the cold wind racing around outside.

It didn't take long for Donna to speak;

"I sense the presence of the little girl. She is very shy and is outside in the hall. She is afraid to come in."

I turned slowly to try to get a look at Lucy one more time. I expected her to be peeking around the corner, but she was not there. I tried to focus around the same area of her height, but she still did not appear. Shortly after Donna announced Lucy's presence, she announced her departure.

The rest of the hour we spent there revealed no other spirits. The house was silent and cold.

Our sessions at home were more successful when we all explored the auras around our heads. Some of us saw bright colors telling us that we had many powers stored within. The night we examined past lives became very emotional, as some could not go there, fearing an unstable reaction. If anything, this winter classes were very entertaining and created new friendships.

Back at the Barnstable House, Donna decided to give up the search for contacting spirits. Either we were too cold to concentrate or the ghost had no interest in us that night. We left disappointed, but I enjoyed the return visit. I'm sure the house and its permanent guest were laughing as we drove away.

Chapter 16

Other Occurrences Before And After Halloween 1985

File #1

On 30 October, 1985, Yankee Homes magazine stated that many phone calls regarding the sale of the Barnstable House and property were disrupted several times with the operator cutting in saying that the phone was now disconnected or that the party had reached the wrong number, or the callers could not contact the owner by phone. Was the ghost trying to stop the sale of the house?

In one very interesting case, a person that did answer the phone said that the Barnstable House had burnt down! Legend has it that all the glass doorknobs in one upstairs bedroom are the main passageways for the spirits to enter the house from the other world.

Another report said that the two upstairs bedrooms and attic was the scene of three murders. This same source states that Thomas Paine; brother of Robert who signed the Declaration of Independence was the first owner of the house. This statement conflicts with the findings that James Paine was the owner of the house. Either way, the Paine family did build the house.

In another reported case; Psychic, Sybil Leek had a seance in the house and reported that eleven ghost lived there. One named Sarah who was the wife of the sea captain that drowned at sea, and whose daughter is supposedly, Lucy who drowned in the spring in the basement.

File #2

On one occasion, a realtor drove to the Cape one day to see the house. It was a very pretty, sunny, and clear day when he started out. A heavy rain poured down from nowhere. It was the first rain in many months for that summer. Cautiously, he finally made it to the house, but when he got out of the car, the weather had turned very cold and wintry. He heard the shutters starting to slam against the side of the house. He waited for the owner to arrive. Again, the shutters were making such a noise that the realtor turns to see them. To his surprise, there were no shutters on the house.

He now was very concerned about what was happening around him, but that was not scary enough to stop him in seeing the house. When the owner did arrive, he told the realtor that there were three murders that were committed upstairs. A very cold breeze shot right through him as he was escorted during his tour. Jack Fitzgerald had a very chilling experience as a realtor that day.

File #3

In 1988, this author entered the house once again. This time, not as a psychic researcher with Donna Miller, but as a person curious about that status of the house. It was under construction once again in its long history. The doors were ripped off their hinges; walls were torn down as we stepped over the rubble to the dinning room. As I looked around, I thought of the many sightings that took place, and that were documented. We explored further until I stood at the foot of the stairs leading up to all the many other encounters.

Up there, is where I spotted Lucy who played with her ball and with me as she peeked around the closet door at me. I couldn't help but to leave my small search party and go up to that small bedroom where I first saw her. The sounds of my friend's voices faded as I climbed higher upstairs. Except for all the debris, it still looked the same. Dark walls, narrow passageways, and low ceilings. I silently slipped away to the third floor.

At first, I peeked into the familiar room. It was empty and had the same feeling as that night. The workmen had not started any work in there, so everything appeared the same. The homemade doors to the closets were gone, and I slowly approached the one closet I was interested in.

I stood there and stared at the entrance hoping to get a glimpse of Lucy once again. Even though it was daylight, the inside of the closet was very dark. I took a close look into its black opening. Suddenly, I saw something! It was a small object not more then ten feet from me. The atmosphere became eerie and strange as I got down on my hands and knees. I slowly crawled to examine my discovery.

I was suddenly taken back in shock! My blood drained, and a big chill came over me. I thought it to be fear, but then I got control of myself and reassessed my find. A broad smile ran across my face as I reached out for the object. I felt a warmth take over my body as I held it close to me. For a few seconds this sacred icon was my treasure of joy!

Did I finally communicate with little Lucy? Her spirit was with me! I was sure of it! Three years before, she reached out to me. Now, I was holding the dearest thing close to me. There in my hands nestled against my chest was a small blue inflated rubber ball about eight inches in diameter. I could not believe what I was holding!

After standing there for a few seconds, I quickly ran downstairs to share my find with the others. My wife, Leslie, was the other person there that night with Donna, and when she saw what I had in my hands, her blood drained. Our two friends, Tom and Colleen knew the story and upon reminding them of it, they too were taken by surprise.

Like four little children, we closely examined the ball, passing to each other, maybe trying to see or get some spiritual message or feeling. I took the treasure from my playmates, and my look told them I could not bring this fantastic find home with me.

I slowly went over to the stairs and walked back up to the third floor room. I stood there again in the center of the room and looked around one last time. I moved over to the closet, peeked in and studied the blue ball again. I smiled and tossed the ball back into the closet, calling out to Lucy;

"Here Lucy! I want you to keep this!…….. Good Bye!"

I walked out of the room for the last time, and we all left the building, never to return again.

File #4

The house was on sale for $350,000 in 1988, but was recorded later as selling for $940,000 in 1989. Located on 1.5 acres with one out building, two lots across the street, a parking lot that parks twenty cars. The high weeds and disrepair took away from the grand historical stature. Off the main chimney connected six fireplaces, five of them working. The bar at the back of the building was nearly condemned.

As the new owners rebuilt, the house stayed empty for a couple of years. A new look and shape took place as the dinning room, bedrooms, and living rooms became offices. Thousands of dollars were pumped back into its veins, giving it new life for the next generation.

File #5

In October 1989 at 11:20 PM, on TV Channel 58, The Dusty Rhodes TV Show tried to sensationalize the house once more by having Mr. Mathews who was one of the eight firemen who saw the ghost in the 1970's visit his show on location at the house.

Upstairs, Dusty held a flashlight trying to induce a dramatization to create an eerie sight for the viewers. Again, the event was kicking off the Halloween season. No spirits came forth that night. Maybe they are accustom to Hollywood and their attempts to bring them out.

The Legend Continues Today

After June, in 1998, "Chronicle" the TV show on Channel 5 hosted by Mary Richardson presented an episode on "Cape Cod Mysteries" which included a segment on the Barnstable House. The following is what the people who were interviewed noted.

Some classical vintage photographs of the house were displayed. They claimed it was built in 1716 and that the ghosts enjoy spending the winter and summers there. They even claimed that the house was once used as a brothel and contained eleven ghosts. One, a little girl of ten years old who drowned in the basement spring, and now walks around with her mother. Little Lucy also playfully runs around the house. There are also other spirits living in the basement including Dr. Savage who was of a strange nature, always cranky. In the later seventeen hundreds they said he hung himself in the house, claimed Robert Brown, attorney and historian practicing at the house today.

Robert Brown says that Robert Treat Paine who was one of the signers of the Declaration of Independence was related to James Paine, the builder of the house.

Chronicle interviewed present owner Jane Richardi who said one attorney got upset over his Harvard rocker always rocking by itself while he was trying to conduct business with clients. One day he was so upset that he picked it up and through it out the door.

Another interview was with a previous waitress at the Barnstable House who now lives in Las Vegas. She said the little girl used to appear all the time and that old broken clocks use to start ticking for no reason. She added that groaning voices were always heard coming through the walls. Many restaurant employees have quit over the ghosts.

Barnstable Fire Chief John Jenkins recalled their experience over 25 years ago when three of his firemen spotted the lady in the wedding dress during a fire call to the house. She was upstairs crying for help, but when they went up to investigate, no one was there. Some of the firemen claimed that they talked with her in the parking lot. Today, Chief Jenkins drives by and always looks up to the windows hoping to get a glimpse of the lady. He thinks about the encounter all the time.

The limited tour of the house on Chronicle showed a beautifully restored Barnstable House, and the present owners should be commended on such a fine job done on one of the finished historical homes in Barnstable.

28 Oct. 1999

In keeping with tradition, the Cape Cod Times Newspaper is probably the most faithful fan of the Barnstable House. A very descriptive and romantically gothic article was written on this day by Kate Robotham, Contributing Writer for the paper. Upon the history of the house we find this version given:

"Built with pre-cut lumber which was sailed to Barnstable from Scituate around 1716, the building was initially owned by James Paine whose grandson, Robert Paine, was destine to sign the Declaration of Independence. Edmund Hawes bought the home and then sold it to Elisha Doane who paid for the building with Continental currency – which was worthless by the end of the American Revolution.

By the late 1700's, the house had become the property of an eccentric (some claim evil) physician, Dr. Samuel Savage. He sold it to Abner Davis, whose wife inherited the house upon his death in 1839. Captain John Grey lived in the house during widow Nancy Davis reign as owner.

During this century, the building has been an inn, a restaurant and an office building, going by the names the 1716 House, the Old Jail House, Capt. Grey's, the Sign of the Blue Lantern, the Old Barnstable Tavern and the Andrea Doria Inn."

This report claims there is a waiter ghost:

"Some people were eating in the restaurant when it was the Old Barnstable Tavern and saw a guy walk by them, dressed in old colonial clothes, from one part of the restaurant into the pub. He looked like a waiter with a towel over his arm. The guest went up to the bartender and said how cool it was to have people dressed up like that and the bartender thought he was crazy. There were no waiters dressed up."

Another account of the research results of Katie Atanian, age 13 at the time and her friend and co-researcher Devon, age 16. They recall the lady with the Barnstable Firefighters. They said she was "a lady (Who) was seen smoking up in the attic when the fire broke out." The girls went up there one day to investigate and found several cigarette butts laying around on the floor.

When Devon went down to the basement to look around she came "face to face with the original owner's daughter, 7 year old Lucy Paine (age varies with reporters and last name not verified), who lost her life in the cellar well in the 1700's. Lucy's mother has also been seen rocking in the living room rocker. She wanders around looking for her "mischievous Lucy." Both not knowing they are ghost within the walls of the Barnstable House.

The stories about Captain Grey never end as he is accused of being a poltergeist and in need of attention and has an attitude problem. His favorite place is the cellar and often slams doors throughout the house.

Poor Edmund Hawes hung himself outback on a tree in 1783 after his worthless Continental money was revealed. He too hangs (didn't mean the pun on words) around the cellar and surely hates to deal with Captain Grey's moods

A ghostbuster, Petronelle Cook of Cape Cod has investigated several stories of the "Phantom fires" that appear in the fireplaces, as did this author did during the 1985 Halloween Party night. Cook has taught anthropology classes at the Cape Cod Community College on spiritual behavior. She thinks that the Cape cod climate has something to do with attracting spirits to our shores. She adds that "Nantucket is crawling with ghosts."[2]

---

[2] Time Stands Still for Certain Cape Cod Residents, Cape Cod Times 28 Oct. 1999 by Kate Robotham

More Recordings

26 Oct. 2000

Recorded from the Barnstable Patriot Newspaper we have the story continue to be kept alive as they mention the young girl who drowned, giving her name as Lucy. They state that 11 ghosts dwell in the Barnstable House. After being a "private home, an inn and a restaurant it is now converted to offices, "mostly for attorney's, in the early 1980's."

They report that not much has happened "aside from a rocking chair that occasionally rocks on its own or, as is said, by Lucy's mother."

The mention of the 1974 sighting by the West Barnstable firefighters one late winter night of "a woman with long blonde hair and a white gown amidst the smoke and flames in a third-story window, but when they went to rescue her she was nowhere to be found.

Following that, several firefighters said they saw the woman outside allegedly hovering two feet above the snow, but she disappeared before anyone could reach her."

They go on to mention the existence of "Edmund Howe who hanged himself from a tree in the yard during the Revolutionary War," and the ghost of "Captain Graves who haunts the cellar, and who sold the house before he died to Doctor Savage." The astonishing mention that poor Doctor

Savage was "considered a practitioner of the black arts." Has time made these poor souls into demons?

Lucy is said to be seen "skipping around the dining room table, and her mother, who some claim awaits her daughter's return, apparently unaware of Lucy's presence in the house."

When property manager Robert Scales of Clark Engineered Products who has an office in the building, recalls the tales, he does so with a "typical Yankee skepticism." When asked if he had any spooky experiences he humorously replied;

"No! Not really. It's all in the eyes of the beholder."

Nov. 2002
Cape Cod Travel advertised in their feature stories, "The Spirits of Cape Cod" that the 1716 Barnstable House is one place to note during the hunt for spirits on the Cape.

"In 1974, a fire broke out in the building during a winter snowstorm. The Barnstable Fire Department arrived on the scene to save this historic building. When they arrived, the witnessed a blond woman in one of the upstairs rooms dressed in 1900's apparel. Once the firefighters reached the room, the woman completely disappeared. No body was ever found."

Today, the curious still drive by, coming from as far away as England and other places around the world, hoping to get a glimpse of a ghost. Some, who know the stories, point upstairs to the windows telling the tale of the bride, and the fires. The house just sits there, looking down at all the tourists telling the ghost stories to each other.

Don't get too close! You could get sucked up into its walls for eternity!

The Dining Room where many ghosts appeared

Chapter 17

Historical Facts About The Barnstable House

(Owners & Renters Who Contributed To The Spirit Of The House)

This list has been taken from records from the Barnstable Court House, The Sturgis Library in Barnstable, newspapers and magazine accounts. Some interviews were mistaken when managers were introduced as owners, but in every case, all people listed in this book were real participants of the reported events, including "ALL THE GHOST!"

1. 1714 to c. 1775, James and or Thomas and Robert Paine (Payne) built the house in Scituate and moved it to Barnstable, Massachusetts. Not listed in Barnstable county records (possibly destroyed by fire).

2. 1775 to c. 1803, Elisha Doane, the father of Hope Doane who married Dr. Samuel Savage, Harvard Educated doctor practicing in Barnstable.

3. ? to 1777, Mr. Edmund Howes listed as selling the house in 1777, but this record is not listed in Barnstable county records (possibly destroyed by fire).

4. 1777 to c. 1790's, Daniel A. Davis. Historical account says he owned the house, but there is no listing in Barnstable county records (possibly destroyed by fire).

5. 1775 to c. 1803, Doctor Samuel Savage was probably a renting tenant of his father-in-law, Elisha Doane.

6. 1803 to c. 1803, Daniel Davis and John Davis were probable children of Daniel A. Davis. They took over the property or bought it from his estate after he died (Found in Barnstable county record book #2, page 197).

7. 1803 to 7 January 1832, William H. and Charles Savage, probable relations to Dr. Samuel Savage took possession of the house (Found in Barnstable county record book #11, page 41).

8. 1832 to 1926. It is not clear if the ownership was in the hands of the Savage family.

9. ? to 1926. Paul M. and Gladys P. Swift are listed as owning the house (Found in Barnstable county records book #413, page 412, dated 12 November 1926).

10. 1926 to 25 February 1927. Thomas Otis owned the house and called it "The Blue Tavern." It was listed under "The Blue Tavern Corporation." This corporation went bankrupt (Found in Barnstable county records book #444, page 160).

11. 25 February 1927. Harold A. and Ethelp Daggett took possession of the house. It is not positive if they were partners with Thomas Otis or if they were administrators of the property (Found in Barnstable county records book #444, page 160).

12. 1920's to 1930's. Adolphus Davis, a Boston ship builder is listed as an owner, but no county record available (records possibly destroyed by fire).

13. 1920's to 1930's. Governor of Massachusetts (name unknown) is listed as an owner, bur records not available (Possibly destroyed by fire).

14. ? to 7 December 1945. Elmer E. Clapp bought the house at a bankrupt auction from the above Thomas Otis bankruptcy. (Found in Barnstable County records book #638, page 446).

15. 1945 to 25 February 1949. Clarence and Mabel Whipple Bangs owned the house (Found in Barnstable county records book #774, page 413).

16. 1949 to 1 March 1953. Lucia S. Nielson owned the house. (Found in Barnstable county records, grantee indexes 1955 M-Z, and book #1233, page 107).

17. 1953 to 19 December 1955. Ray H. Orde owned the house (Found in Barnstable county records book, but no number listed).

18. 1955 to 9 January 1964. Lennart A. and Linnea K. Svensson owned the house (Found in Barnstable county records book #1360, page 796).

19. 1964 to? Jack J. Furman owned the house. (Found in Barnstable county records book #2016, page 082).

20. ? to 20 July 1971. Janet G. Johnson was listed as an owner (Found in Barnstable county records book #2016, page 080).

21. 1971 to 20 May 1975. Nellie Marsden DeAngelis owned the house (Found in Barnstable county records book #2736, page 112).

22. 1975 to 26 June 1978. Robert F. Lilly was owner of the house (Found in Barnstable county records book #3254, page 165).

23. 1975 to c. 1978. Eleanor H. Humphreys was possibly partner in ownership with Robert Lilly (Found in Barnstable county records book #3254, page 165).

24. 1978 to c. 1981. Richard Lindstedt was said to be the owner, but there is no county record found.

25. 1978 to 17 March 1981. Glenn E. Shealey was owner of the house (Found in Barnstable county records book #4749).

26. 31 Dec. 1984. John G. Fitzgerald took out a Common Victualler's License (Liquor) to operate the Barnstable House, which had an address of 3010 Main Street in Barnstable. This license was not valid unless used in conjunction with a food permit. The fee was $50 and the licensing authorities that were the Board of Selectmen signed the document that was good until 31 Dec. 1985. This owner was gracious enough to allow the radio station, Donna Miller and this author access to the building during the "1985 Halloween Party" that help bring this book to reality.

27. 1985 to 9 October 1988. John G. Fitzgerald owned the house (Found in Barnstable county records book #4749, page 121).

28. 1988 to possibly the present. George W. Blakely owns the house. (Found in Barnstable county records book #6215, page 10).

Note:
There is no listing for a Captain Grey/Gray or Graves as being an owner of the house. Because of the nature and availability of some records, the dates and time span of ownership may be in question.

Today, we all know who the real owner of the Barnstable House!

The Tree!

Surname Index

Anderson, viii, 32
Atanian, 77
Bangs, 31(2), 81
Benjamin, 21
Blakely, 82
Bourne, 69
Brown, 75(2)
Bunnell/Bonnell, iv(4), vi (2), viii
Carlson, viii, 6, 11
Clapp, 31(2), 81
Cobb, 20(2)
Cook, 78(2)
Cox, viii, 48
Crocker, 16(2)
Crosby, 15(2)
Crowell, 29
Curry, 33(3)
Daggett, 31(2), 81
Davis, 11, 16(6), 17(2), 18(2), 19(4), 20(23), 29(2), 30(6), 31, 77(2), 80(4), 81
DeAngelis, 82
Deyo, viii

Doane, 16, 22(2), 76, 80(3)
Emmes, 5
Farnes, 16
Fitzgerald, vii, 30, 33(2), 73, 82(2)
Fonda, 62
Freeman, 15, 16, 21
Friss, vii
Frost, viii, 32
Furman, 32(2), 81
Gale, 26, 28
George (King) III, 12
Gorham, 7, 15, 20
Goss, vii
Gray/Grey/Graves, 29(9), 30(4), 77(4), 78, 82
Hall, 15(2), 16
Holmes, 26
Holt, 16
Holzer, 32(2), 45
Howes/Hawes, 12(3), 14(7), 15(15), 16(3), 76, 77, 78, 80
Humphreys, 82

Jenkins, 76(2)
Johnson, 33(2), 34, 82
Jones, 39(2)
Knapp, 26(2)
Lathrop, 20(4)
Lauren & Wallie, viii, 50, 57, 65, 67, 68
Leek, 32(2), 45, 72
Lewis, 21, 60
Lilly, 82(2)
Lindstedt, 43, 46, 47, 63, 82
Lincoln, 27
Little, vii
Loring, 24
Lorrigon, 47
Lynch, iv
Matthews, 15, 75
Melville, 22, 26(6), 27(6), 28(2), 33, 69
McCoy, iv
Miller, iv(2), vi, vii, 52, 55, 67, 68, 73, 82
Morrie, 61
Mumford, 5
Neilson, 32(2), 33, 81
Orde, 32(2), 81
Otis, 16(4), 31(3), 81(3)
Paine/Payne, 1(5), 2(2), 3(3), 4(3), 5(14), 6(18), 7, 11(2), 16(2), 30, 69(3), 72(3), 75(2), 76(2), 77, 78, 80(2)
Page, iii
Rhodes, viii, 75
Rich, 22
Richardi, 76
Richardson, 75

Robotham, 76, 78
Rogers, 22
Rymanowski, viii
Sarducci, 60, 61
Savage, 21(4), 22(2), 23(2), 24(5), 25(5), 27, 29, 30(2), 69, 75, 77, 78(2), 80(4), 81
Sears, 15(3)
Scales, 79
Shaw, 22(2), 26(5), 27(5)
Shealey, 82
Slovan, 65, 68
Smith, 16(2)
Snow, 6
Sprague, vii, 30
Sturgis, 11, 16, 28
Svenson, 32(2), 81
Swift, 30(2), 81
Taylor, 11
Thatcher/Thacher, 5(2), 7(2), 17(2), 23(3), 24
Tryser/Trayser, vii, 26
Tyler, 21, 22
Waitt, 16
Webster, 27
Winslow, 7
Wood, vii, 22(2)
Wyatt, iv (2)
Vuilleumier, vii (2), viii, 32
Yound, 24

ABOUT THE AUTHOR

Paul J. Bunnell, FACG, UE

Loyalty is Everything

For the past twenty-five years, Paul has devoted himself to genealogy and Loyalist studies. Self educated, he later took credited classes from Brigham Young University of Provo, Utah, greatly improving his skills and knowledge in this field. His accomplishments are wide; awarded the Accreditation and Fellowship at the American College of Genealogists of Illinois, and certified and registered lineage member of the United Empire Loyalist Association of Canada, and The Hereditary Order of Descendants of the Loyalists and Patriots of the American Revolution. He has held past and present memberships in over sixty genealogical and writing organizations around the world, including life long memberships and chairman positions. He is also certified with the International Ghost Hunters Society in Paranormal Investigation, and also as a Ghost Hunter. He is a registered BYU blood donor on their genealogical DNA study. His speaking engagements have been in New Jersey, New York, Massachusetts, New Hampshire, Maine, Connecticut and New Brunswick, including TV interviews on Cape Cod, Massachusetts, and Saint John, New Brunswick. In 1989, His Majesty The Prince Philip of Wales (England) accepted his book, Thunder Over New England—Benjamin Bonnell, the Loyalist, at Buckingham Palace. He was also presented with the famous "Loyalist Pin" from the past mayor, Elsie Wayne of Saint John, New Brunswick, Canada (The Loyalist City). Paul has also produced several Internet articles on genealogy, including "Black Loyalist," and "Bonnell/Bunnell Loyalists." And, let's not forget the "Loyalist Ghost of Benjamin Bonnell." Future publications: Life of a Haunted House; The Barnstable House; Tumbleweed; The Nellie Markham Letters; New Loyalist Index, Vol. 4; Native North American and French Marriages; and many other books in progress. Paul enjoys traveling around lecturing or selling books at his vendor table at conventions. He also does Loyalist research for others out of his very large home library.

Other Heritage Books by Paul J. Bunnell:

Cemetery Inscriptions of the Town of Barnstable, Massachusetts, and Its Villages, 1600-1900

Cemetery Inscriptions of the Town of Barnstable, Massachusetts, and Its Villages, 1600-1900, with Corrections and Additions

French and Native North American Marriages, 1600-1800

Life of a Haunted House—The Barnstable House of Barnstable, Massachusetts: Genealogy of a Real Haunted House

Research Guide to Loyalist Ancestors: A Directory to Archives, Manuscripts, and Published Sources

Research Guide to Loyalist Ancestors: A Directory to Archives, Manuscripts, Published and Electronic Sources (Updated and Revised)

The House of Robinson—The Robinsons of Rhode Island: Their Genealogy and Letters, and the History of the Robinson & Son Oil Company of Baltimore, Maryland

The New Loyalist Index, Volume I

The New Loyalist Index, Volume II

The New Loyalist Index, Volume III: Including Cape Cod and Islands, Massachusetts, New Hampshire, New Jersey and New York Loyalists

Thunder Over New England—Benjamin Bonnell, the Loyalist: A Loyalist Story and Family Genealogy, Including Other Loyalist Bunnell/Bonnell Genealogies Revised and Updated

www.ingramcontent.com/pod-product-compliance
Lightning Source LLC
Chambersburg PA
CBHW071435160426
43195CB00013B/1911